Jeff has a remarkable personal story of God's grace and he has lived what he teaches. His personal journey from poverty to success should be an encouragement to all of us that all things are possible with God. I thoroughly endorse his holistic approach and I highly recommend this book. It is a resource that deserves to be widely read.

Gary Clarke, Lead Pastor, Hillsong London

Jeff has a fantastic view of money and possessions because of his deep biblical understanding. In his book, *True Riches*, he not only provides education, he gives revelation. I wish all people in the Body of Christ would grasp the amazing blessings from the Lord when we walk with Him in our finances. All of Jeff's teachings have been earned through experience. He not only has the talk, he has the walk. This book is a game changer.

Gunnar Johnson, Executive Pastor of Stewardship, Gateway Church, Director of Generosity, The King's University, Southlake, Texas

History teaches that the committed always conquer the complacent and how the rituals and restraints of religion build commitment. By boldly brandishing the banner of faith in the arena of wealth creation, my dear friend and respected business professional, Jeff Lestz, reveals the road map to real riches. Every page of this volume carries valuable insights which will help bring about fiscal transformation in the life of every reader.

Rabbi Daniel Lapin, radio and television personality and author of *Thou Shall Prosper*

True Riches is one of the best books I have read on biblical finances. It not only provides the reader with an excellent foundation on what the Bible teaches about money but offers some very practical strategies that can help you on your journey to achieving your life's goals. I found this to be a thoroughly enjoyable read that reflects the author's mission and passion to help others attain financial freedom.

George Aghajanian, General Manager Hillsong Church, Australia

In this refreshing book, Jeff challenges us to be purposeful with our finances, inspires us through his own incredible life journey, and equips us with the tools and mindset to live out financially healthy lives.

Dr Rebecca Newton, Business Psychologist

Jeff Lestz is a storyteller, he tells the story of his own life and how God has blessed his life. He tells stories from the Bible that help us understand that blessing. But best of all, he tells the story of economic truth based on scriptural principles. God has an economic system that works and will work, in any area of life. What Jeff does in this great book is help us see these truths in clear, scriptural common sense.

Dr Scott Wilson (President Eurolead.net. Director ICLM)

The combination of financial with spiritual education is essential in today's world. I have thoroughly enjoyed reading *True Riches*, finding its content balanced and enlightening with both spiritual and practical wisdom. Jeff Lestz's knowledge and experience shine through on every page. If you apply the principles contained in this book, your life will surely change for the better.

Ashley Schmierer, Christian Outreach Centre International President

Jeff has produced a must-read for all Christians. His down-to-earth and easy writing style is biblical, balanced and practical. In these last days, we need Christians in the marketplace and all spheres of life to have a healthy view of money and financial stewardship. I believe this book will empower you with the principles to get wealthier . . . for the right reasons!

Dr Jonathan Oloyede, National Day of Prayer and Worship

I can tell you for certain, Jeff Lestz is for real. This book is written by a guy who lives it. This is not some theoretical approach from someone who does not have real world experience applying these biblical concepts. These principles have worked in Jeff's life. I have seen it; they have worked in my life; they will work in your life!

Bob Safford Jr., Co-CEO Genistar Limited

Jeff Lestz is one of the few people I know whose passion to empower people to experience financial freedom knows no bounds. This book is a part of that expression, in which he shares practical God-given wisdom not simply to get out of debt but to take that next step into living a life free from undue financial pressure. Here the crossroads of ancient Jewish wisdom interface with contemporary Christian thinking.

Rev. Nims Obunge, MBE DL, CEO Peace Alliance, London, UK

The thing I like about Jeff Lestz is that he is quietly rich. He doesn't drive around in a big flashy car or wear flashy clothes (they never look that flashy!). He's frugal. No big brands. No obvious insecurities. He's not 'Get Rich Quick' and he's not in love with the stuff. BUT he is rich. He is a rare spirit that is proving to be the right spirit for this hour. He's down to earth, loves people a lot, is faith-filled and out to lift a generation out of debt and lack into abundance and generosity. This book could actually change your life. I like Jeff. I like him a lot. And you will too after this great read.

Dave Gilpin, Senior Pastor, Hope City Church, Sheffield, UK

Money, the M word, it's one of those hot potato topics that some people would rather us not talk about and therein lies a problem. Money is such an integral part of every person's life and matters so much to our health and well being that God chooses not to ignore it and speaks about it, therefore so should we. In this book *True Riches*, Jeff Lestz presents an exceptional, biblically holistic view regarding money. This book is written by a man who wants you to do well financially, that alone makes it worth the read. I thoroughly recommend it.

Paul Benger, Senior Pastor, Christian Life Church, Chesterfield, UK

True Riches will give you the tools to live a generous and blessed life. Jeff's holistic approach is refreshing and will definitely fast-track your finances.

Dr Simone Laubscher, Rejuv

If you meet Jeff you may think that his passion is finance. It is not. He is passionate about people and seeing them released into freedom through Christ, then into financial freedom. Jeff shows how to unsqueeze ourselves from a worldly pattern of thinking on money and transform our thinking into a biblical model. As a pastor of a church I would recommend this book to all our community and to you.

Jon Cook, Senior Pastor, Newcastle Christian Life Centre, UK

I have been studying Bible economics for over 20 years. Having read this book of Jeff Lestz I am encouraged and informed by the solid exegesis of biblical text. There are decades of wisdom in this this book, that will empower both those struggling financially and those who have developed a clear financial plan for life, to succeed in a greater dimension. I would highly recommend a copy of this book be read by parents and a copy to be bought for all their children over 16 years old.

Ian Green, Executive Director Proton Foundation and Ian Green Communications

Jeff Lestz is a legend! Seemingly for a while everywhere I went I kept hearing his name and was asked had I read his book or heard him speak. Now having heard him speak and read his book I know why he came so highly recommended.

Jeff has an ability to take ancient truth and apply it to the modern world. He speaks and writes with clarity and conviction drawing you in to prove for yourself that these principles have lasted through time and that they still work today. The gift of a teacher is often described as the ability to make the complex simple. Jeff does this about a subject that too many fear to examine.

His book is practical, principled and in plain English which makes it accessible to all and a must-read for everyone.

Steve Campbell, Senior Pastor, C3 Church, Cambridge, UK

Those who learn to handle money correctly and righteously will make the most of life. It is by wisdom that good wealth is built and in this book, Jeff puts that wisdom in your hands. Here you will learn that life is not about money, but money matters to life. Read this book now. Learn the principle now. Practise it now. Then give a copy to people you care about.

Tope Koleoso, Senior Pastor, Jubilee Church London

True Riches is a practical, accessible book for ordinary people who are looking for wisdom in handling finance. As a family we have evidence of this wisdom. One shared thought from Jeff saw a radical shift in our finances which has led to new levels of future security.

Stuart Bell, Senior Pastor, Alive Church and Leader of the Ground Level Network of Churches

Jeff has spoken at !Audacious on several occasions – he's an incredibly relational person. As a Bible economist he will inspire you and your church to truly understand the nature and character of finance. As a speaker he is motivational, encouraging and inspiring but he'll also give insight into areas of finance that many people will never have seen or understood before. His insight is incredibly releasing and empowering.

Glyn Barrett, Senior Pastor, !Audacious Church, Manchester, England

True Riches

Jeff Lestz

A CIP record for this book is available from the British Library.

First edition 2013, reprinted 2015

Unless otherwise stated, all Scripture quotations are from The Holy Bible, New King James Version. Copyright © 1982 by Thomas Nelson, Inc.

Other versions used:
NIV – The Holy Bible, New International Version®, NIV® Copyright © 1973, 1978, 1984, 2011 by Biblica, Inc.® Used by permission. All rights reserved worldwide.

GNT – Good News Translation. Copyright © 1992 by American Bible Society.

The Message – Copyright © 1993, 1994, 1995, 1996, 2000, 2001, 2002 by Eugene H. Peterson.

ISBN: 978-1-90599-162-4

Cover design by SpiffingCovers – www.spiffingcovers.com
Typeset by CRB Associates, Potterhanworth, Lincolnshire
Printed in the United Kingdom

Contents

Foreword

The issue of finance is a subject that occupies the minds of most people, most of the time. Yet, for all the 'thinking time' we give to money, it is still the one area in life open to the most confusion. People are constantly trying to figure out smarter, better ways of making money, managing their finances and planning for the future – with mixed success.

Transfer this common dilemma into the arena of the Christian life, and the problem becomes worse rather than better. Even though Christians may understand some basic principles of stewardship and conduct their affairs with integrity, many remain confused about what the Bible teaches on handling their finances. Added to this, there is a naivety that exists among some believers who think that God will take care of their financial planning without them having to do anything.

This is where my friend Jeff Lestz's book comes into its own. For more than thirty years Jeff has been educating people on what the Bible has to say about finance and how its truth can be applied to everyday life. In this book he gives us clarity on the misunderstood and often mistaught subject of prosperity.

Jeff presents us with clear, biblically sound financial principles and dispels a number of commonly held myths. He doesn't shy away from dealing with the controversial issues, but responds with words, distilled over many years, that resound with truth and 'tried and tested' experience. Jeff brings the biblical and the practical together into a single, cohesive message.

I love Jeff's approach to teaching about finance, because finance is just a small part of the bigger picture! He has grasped the truth that finance is just one facet of our spiritual life and it must function in harmony with the rest. Jeff has a remarkable personal story of God's grace and he has lived what he teaches. His personal journey from poverty to success should be an encouragement to all of us that all things are possible with God.

I thoroughly endorse his holistic approach and I highly recommend this book. It is a resource that deserves to be widely read.

Gary Clarke
Lead Pastor
Hillsong London

Introduction

I love the local church and pastors! I love people, and see the people in church as my extended family. It motivates me seeing people grow and blossom into something bigger than they could ever imagine.

As you will read in this book, my life changed when I accepted Jesus in my life and became part of a strong, Bible-believing church that wanted to reach out to help people improve their lives. My pastor became my friend, coach and mentor. In more than forty years I have only been a member of three churches and every pastor was special to me.

I have worked with pastors from all over the world and love coming alongside them to help them build the vision that they have for their community. These are men and women who have 'feet of clay' and are human like all of us. Sometimes we put them on too high a pedestal, and when their humanity comes out it crushes our confidence. Let's remember to look to the Chief Pastor, Jesus, but realise that these earthly pastors need our love, respect and support.

My ministry is finance, and it is one of the touchiest subjects around. It always amuses me to hear someone say, 'All the church ever talks about is money', when the only thing they heard about money was during three minutes on a Sunday morning when the offering was being received.

I heard someone else say, 'All the church wants is my money.' I responded and said, 'Actually, the church is the only place I know that is interested in your entire person! Church is about the total development of us in our spiritual, financial, health and relational lives. The church is supposed to care about our lives holistically. Now, last time you went into McDonalds, all they were interested in was your money! I doubt they said with that Big Mac and fries, "Would you like to discuss how the rest of your life is going?"'

So, let's get real now and talk about a touchy subject – Money.

Let me ask you a question. Have you either thought about or spoken about money in the last twenty-four hours? If the answer is no, I believe you're in a minority. For most people, thinking about, speaking about and probably worrying about money occupies a great deal of their time.

It's not surprising then, that money is something that God has a great deal to say about in the Bible. In fact, we find his wisdom on handling finances threaded throughout the Scriptures. It is a constant theme. The proper, biblical stewardship of money is an important issue to God.

Why? Because – as I hope you will learn through this book – once we settle the issue of how to handle money, it opens the door for God to bless us in every other area of our lives. People are reluctant to discuss money because it is taboo, but it's time to break the silence on finances.

Throughout this book we will explore what the Bible has to say about money. There are a number of other books on the market that focus on this – many of which talk about 'prosperity' while only focusing on the financial aspect of our lives. To say prosperity is about money is not an incorrect statement, but it is incomplete.

This book takes a different approach. Although I believe the Bible teaches the centrality of money in everyday life, and coaches us on how to handle it correctly, here we are concerned with the bigger picture of enjoying God's peace and prosperity in the *whole of our lives*.

It is a holistic and, I believe, thoroughly biblical approach. After tackling what the Bible has to say about money, we will go on to look at some of the principles of financial management that I have learned over the years. These, I hope, will help you to navigate towards a place of strength and prosperity for the future.

CHAPTER 1

The Start of a Journey

Before we get started, I want to share my personal story with you. Many years ago, God took hold of my life and set me on a journey. Although I did not know it when I began, the journey was towards financial independence and its purpose was for me to become a blessing to others. I learned a great deal. What I learned and why it is important will, I hope, help you to better understand the principles I share in this book.

I was born and raised in Chicago, the youngest of three children in a Jewish family. My father had been very successful in business, but began to face severe financial challenges. He had never had any real financial education, overspent and ended up drowning in debt. Our family home and most of our possessions were sold off and the five of us moved into a tiny two-bedroom flat.

The pressure of this hit my Dad really hard and he plunged into a deep depression from which he never recovered. Sadly, he made the decision to take his own life when I was five years old. Shortly after this my mother, who had been left penniless, had a nervous breakdown. She turned to alcohol to numb the pain and just a few years after my father passed away, she died too.

I was now eight years old with just my older brother and sister remaining in my world, and I was angry with God. I attended Hebrew school and heard stories about this wonderful God who did all these great miracles and delivered his people. But I just could not bring myself to believe that there *was* a God.

After the death of my parents, there followed four years of being shunted in and out of orphanages and foster homes. By the time I reached my twelfth year, I had come to the conclusion that I had nothing worth living for and attempted to commit suicide myself. As a result I was put into 'therapy', which at the time in Chicago meant being treated in the notorious state psychiatric institution, mostly populated by criminally insane men – not a great place for a kid to be. I didn't want to stay there, so I took my fate into my own hands and ran.

I had had enough of the care system. I decided to take my chances on the streets of Chicago. I lived rough in the city for the next two-plus years. The first six months were simply about surviving each day. I spent my time eating scraps out of people's garbage cans and sleeping in alleyways or abandoned cars.

Eventually, I became involved with a bunch of hippies who were into using and selling drugs. After a short time I too was immersed in the city's drug culture – selling drugs on the street and using them too. I was only 13 years old.

About a year later when I was lying on my bed one night, strung out on drugs, I began crying out to God. The tears were pouring down my cheeks as I pleaded, 'God, if you are really real, help me get my life straightened out.'

Two weeks later I hitchhiked 400 miles away down to a small rural town near St. Louis, Missouri, to visit some of the guys who had taken me in off the streets. They had joined a hippie group called the Cosmic Cowboys Commune – which probably tells you all you need to know about it. All four of these young men had also come from Jewish families.

As I arrived there late one night, my friends were sitting together in the front room of a little dilapidated farmhouse, engrossed in a Bible study. To say I was surprised would be an understatement. I asked one of the guys, 'Boy, what have you been smoking now?!' I thought they had all gone crazy. But, one by one they began to share with me how Jesus had changed their lives.

Although I had cried out to God for help, this was not music to my ears. I now believed that, if there was a God, he must hate me – and frankly, the feeling was mutual. *How could a God of love allow my parents to be taken away from me?* I was haunted by this and so many other unanswered questions.

I had no intention of becoming what I regarded as a nutty, Bible-bashing Christian.

Moreover, I said, 'If I would be any religion, I would be Jewish.' One of the guys pointed out Jesus was Jewish but I responded, 'No way was Jesus Jewish! I think he was a Catholic!' Obviously, my biblical understanding was not too deep.

However, Michael Toppel, one of the guys on the commune, invited me to visit a local church with him. Having only ever been to Jewish synagogue, the little Pentecostal church was an eye-opener – more like a rock 'n' roll gig than a service. But as strange as it seemed to me, that night God began a wonderful work of transformation in my life. I was saved and miraculously delivered from the grip of drugs in an instant.

I was now 15 years old. Michael, at just 21 years old, became my foster father and mentor. The pastor of the church also became a great influence in my life. These two men and others in this small community helped me to change my life.

Thus began a period of restoration as God poured his grace into my life. I had a huge revelation right then: *It didn't matter where I had come from, but it did matter where I was going.* My history did not have to become my destiny. I re-started my education and eventually went to university. In high school I met the only other hippie – Margo – and we began dating. At the age of sixteen I had found the love of my life, and as I write we are about to celebrate our 40th wedding anniversary!

While at university, I grew impatient with academia and wanted to get into a career, so I attended an interview at a financial services company that my foster father was working for. As soon as I began, I discovered that I was made for this industry. I excelled at the work and the company was keen to recruit me.

At nineteen years old, with the offer of a good job doing something I seemed to be gifted in, I decided not to finish my university degree and became an independent financial advisor (IFA). I fell in love with helping people with their finances and teaching them about how money works.

I was soon the company's top salesman. From there I moved into management and after five years I knew I wanted my own business, believing that God had more for me as an entrepreneur than as an employee. I wanted to build a better life for my family, but also wanted to see the kingdom of God and my local church prosper.

At the age of twenty-four I realised that I did not want to work for someone else to make them rich. I began to pray for a business opportunity. At a meeting, I encountered a company called A. L. Williams (now Primerica) which did not just sell financial products but believed in helping consumers and doing what is right, one hundred per cent of the time. I also met some great coaches, role models I could look up to. They were not all Christian but many were, and it inspired me that God could do the same for me.

For seven years, I worked hard and continually turned my business over to God as the real CEO. I met so many wonderful people and mentors who helped me to become a better salesperson, manager, and leader with a heart to mentor others. By the time I was thirty-one, I had become a millionaire. It was hard to believe that only a few years earlier, I had no business or real direction to build any kind of financial security.

For now, forgive me for keeping you guessing as to what happened during the intervening years. Let me say this: whether you believe it or not, it is God's will to bless you in every area of your life. I believe it absolutely is God's will. Just consider:

In the Bible there are around five hundred references to faith, and a similar number regarding prayer, but there are several thousand references to money. The majority of the parables that Jesus taught were about money, because he knew that it was a big deal for most people, most of the time. Yet money seems to be a secret or a taboo to discuss in churches.

3 John 1:2 says,

I pray that you may prosper in all things and be in health, just as your soul prospers.

I don't believe that God sees any virtue in us being poor. The word poverty appears in Scripture just fifteen times and always in a negative context. It is not something that God desires. It is not associated with holiness or piety, as some have mistakenly taught.

Compare this with the appearance of the word 'prosper,' which occurs some ninety times in Scripture and always in a positive context. It is God's will for us to prosper, not to languish in poverty. Words like 'increase' and 'riches' occur just as frequently.

Nowhere in the Bible does it say that if we obey God and keep his commandments, he will reward us with poverty. Rather, he promises that we will prosper in *every* area of our lives. If poverty was a blessing, then God would give it to us. But in fact, the Bible marks it out as undesirable. God loves the poor, but nowhere in the Bible does it say he wants us to be poor or that we should pursue poverty.

Many are living under the curse of a poverty mind-set. As we read on, I will show you how to break that curse over your life and learn to flow in the prosperity that God has promised you. With all my heart I believe that God wants to bless you and bring you to a place of financial independence so you can be a blessing to others. Journey with me now and together we'll discover how. God is a loving father who wants you to live the blessed life!

It is more blessed to give than to receive, but how can we give if we do not have something to give? It is actually selfish to want to be poor! How can you help others if you have nothing yourself? When I read God's Word I see permission to prosper, multiply and be successful in every area of our lives, including finance.

Church and finance

The church is the only place I know of that cares about every area of your life. This book is a 'call to arms' for all Bible believers who want to see the kingdom of God advanced in the earth today. It is meant to shine light in the darkest corners of our life and to challenge beliefs about money that have been avoided because they were considered too sensitive.

Where did the idea come from that to be more spiritual is cloaked in poverty? Where did this idea originate that the poorer we are the closer we must be to God? Whoever thought up the idea that if you take a vow of poverty it brings you closer to God?

I believe the enemy has deceived us into believing that God is a God of limited resources, that there is only so much to go around, and that wealth is only for the privileged few. This idea is steeped in a spirit of low self-esteem and lack of faith, because the area of finance affects us in every area of our lives. If the enemy can keep us in a mind-set of poverty and a mentality of lack, then not only are our own lives restricted, but so are the church and our ministry.

The belief that wealth is bad, and that poverty or the act of being poor gives us humility, comes from a false sense of pride. Nowhere in the scriptures do I find justification for us to relish in a spirit of poverty; in fact, I find exactly the opposite. God commands us to be industrious and go forth and multiply in every area of our lives. We are to be fruitful.

When we are fruitful and multiply, it blesses others as well as ourselves. God himself created the heavens and earth and because we are made in his likeness, we are to be creators and contributors also. When everyone prospers it is a good thing. There is nothing wrong with having a nice lifestyle. In fact, God desires you to enter into a place where you have abundance and can help share with others.

Look at this passage from Deuteronomy which shows how it is God who gives wealth. We can't lose sight of the need to be grateful for what he provides, and to honour him with what we have.

Be careful to follow every command I am giving you today, so that you may live and increase and may enter and possess the land that the LORD promised on oath to your forefathers. Remember how the LORD your God led you all the way in the desert these forty years, to humble you and to test you in order to know what was in your heart, whether or not you would keep his commands. He humbled you, causing you to hunger and then feeding you with manna, which neither you nor your fathers had known, to teach you that man does not live on bread alone but on every word that comes from the mouth of the LORD. Your clothes did not wear out and your feet did not swell during these forty years. Know then in your heart that as a man disciplines his son, so the LORD your God disciplines you.

Observe the commands of the LORD your God, walking in his ways and revering him. For the LORD your God is bringing you into a good land – a land with streams and pools of water, with springs flowing in the valleys and hills, a land with wheat and barley, vines and fig trees, pomegranates, olive oil and honey; a land where bread will not be scarce and you will lack nothing; a land where rocks are iron and you can dig copper out of the hills.

When you have eaten and are satisfied, praise the LORD your God for the good land he has given you. Be careful that you do not forget the LORD your God, failing to observe his commands, his laws and his decrees that I am giving you this day. Otherwise, when you eat and are satisfied, when you build fine houses and settle down, and when your herds and flocks grow large and your silver and gold increase and all you have is multiplied, then your heart will become proud and you will forget the LORD your God, who brought you out of Egypt, out of the land of slavery. He led you through the vast and dreadful desert, that thirsty and waterless land, with its venomous snakes and scorpions. He brought you water out of hard rock. He gave you manna to eat in the desert, something your fathers had never known, to humble and to test you so that in the end it might go well with you. You may say to yourself, 'My power and the strength of my hands have produced this wealth for me.' But remember the LORD your God, for it is he who gives you the ability to produce wealth, and so confirms his covenant, which he swore to your forefathers, as it is today.

(Deuteronomy 8:1–18 NIV)

Escaping the poverty trap

Please don't tell me that poverty gives you humility – I can think of better ways to be humble! Humility is meant to be formed internally, not externally. 2 Chronicles 7:14 (NIV) says,

If my people, who are called by my name, will humble themselves and pray and seek my face and turn from their wicked ways, then I will hear from heaven and will forgive their sin and will heal their land.

This is about God's people voluntarily humbling themselves before him.

The results of poverty are hopelessness, helplessness and dependency on the charity of others. As much as we try to solve the 'war on poverty,' feeding people alone will just fill their stomachs for a day. Empowering their souls and imparting self-confidence to do for themselves is the real answer for lifting the spirit of poverty.

Yes, let's help the needy, but let us also break the cycle. If they never learn to provide for themselves and care for others, then next week or next year they will be in the same position. All we have done is delayed the inevitable.

God's presence is exactly the opposite of hopelessness and despair. Christ brought hope, joy and a sense of purpose to our lives. The true spirit of God is about restoration, encouragement and that God has a plan for our lives to be fulfilled.

Satan wants people to believe that poverty and piety go hand in hand. He tells us that being down and out is our future, that God has limited resources and does not care about us. The belief that 'life has dealt me a bad hand' permeates our society. This spirit of helplessness and hopelessness leads to addictions to fill the void, self-harm and all kinds of self-abuse.

I personally was in this pit of despair, poverty and self-pity. I can just about match any 'pity party' story. My father committed suicide when I was five years old. My mother had a nervous breakdown and became an alcoholic, dying a broken and hopeless woman. The only time we spent together was either in a bar where she got drunk, or when she visited me at an orphanage, already drunk.

I had several wealthy aunts and uncles and no one took me in – I was not wanted. I was in and out of six different homes in five years, and at the age of twelve I tried to commit suicide by slashing my wrists. I was shoved into a mental hospital and ran away to live on the streets of Chicago for over two years. I ended up getting into drugs and a gang and at fifteen years old was bitter and in despair about life, on the road to self-destruction. Talk about a messed-up life!

I can describe the spirit it brings: fear, hopelessness, doubt, jealousy and bitterness towards others doing better than me; self-pity, doubt, depression, discouragement, helplessness. I was unable to believe that there was a better future, no matter what I did.

If the enemy can get us in this frame of mind, in a spirit of confusion, lacking personal resources, we will never be able to bless others. This leads to dependency on the state or the church and a sense that 'Life owes me something,' becoming a taker and not a giver. I know this because I hated everything about life. These attributes are NOT God's attributes.

At age fifteen I heard the message of God's eternal love for me. I discovered that through faith in Jesus I could have a relationship with a loving God, a true dad who would care for me. It caused a transformation in my life.

However, I had to work on my attitude. I had to get into God's Word and read some other books on how to improve myself. I began to realize that God really did love me, but it was up to me to take personal responsibility and not expect him to do the things for me that I was capable of.

The attributes of God are empowerment, encouragement, hope in the future, joy, peace, satisfaction, and a desire to create in order to contribute. He gave me a heart to serve others and a sense of real purpose to my life. A sense of adventure and expectation grew, that right around the corner God has another surprise for me!

The belief that there is a better future for me, and that God has a plan for my life, for good and not evil, brings joy. It drives back the dark clouds of doubt, discouragement, disbelief and destruction.

Poverty is about hopelessness and discouragement. By contrast, success, progressing and enjoying the nicer things in life and, being a contributor brings joy, hope, and excitement. It is like a father's love for his children and desire to see them do better. God absolutely wants the best for you!

Flowing in and flowing out

There are two bodies of water in Israel. One is the Jordan River and it has an intake and an outlet. The flow of melted snow from the mountains brings about fish and other wildlife in the water. Why? Because the water is flowing and alive with oxygen and life.

The other body of water is the Dead Sea. Water flows in but there is no outlet. Nothing lives in these waters. It is great for a mud or salt bath but it cannot sustain life. Making money and accumulating wealth is a pretty empty pursuit if it is just to consume or to satisfy your own personal desires, and if there is no deeper purpose to wealth creation.

The Dead Sea represents poverty, or having wealth and not using it for anything beyond our own personal lives. We contribute nothing back. The Jordan River is about abundant life, something growing and alive. As the life flows, the more it gives, the more it seems to get.

So, stand back, enemy! We are getting ready to invade areas of darkness and disbelief and replace them with light. Believe that God has a plan for you, which is to prosper in every single area of your life. Once you get this revelation that it is a good thing to prosper and become more generous, your life will be fuller and you will flow like the Jordan River.

One person gives freely, yet gains even more;
another withholds unduly, but comes to poverty.
A generous person will prosper;
whoever refreshes others will be refreshed.
(Proverbs 11:24–25 NIV)

CHAPTER 2

A Holistic Approach

One of our biggest errors with money is to treat it separately from the other areas of our life. We tend to live compartmentalised lives, especially in the Western world, where we try to manage our relationships, our health, spiritual life and finances in isolation from each other. This is a mistake, and it's completely unbiblical.

God deals with you as a whole person. Contrary to popular belief, he is not interested solely in your spiritual life. He wants to be intimately involved in your relationships, your health and your financial life too. Why? It's because he knows that each area of your life affects all the other areas. He made you that way.

One of the most important messages you can take away from reading this book is that these four areas of life are inextricably linked. In this book I have chosen to focus on the aspect of finance, but not to the exclusion of the other three areas. These four areas are inseparably interwoven together in the fabric of life.

I want to help you understand how finances work as a part of your whole life. It is a holistic approach to thinking about, and dealing with money. God is concerned with your whole life and how all the different elements of it work together. He is interested in blessing you, the *whole person* – in every aspect. Finance is only part of prosperity, not the totality of it.

This truth is illustrated nowhere better than in the sixth chapter of Deuteronomy. Verse four contains the opening words of the *Shema* – the central prayer of the Jewish prayer book. It is often the first section of Scripture that a Jewish child will commit to memory. Special emphasis is placed upon these first six words, *Shema Yisrael, Adonai Eloheinu, Adonia echad,* translated 'Hear, O Israel, the LORD is our God, the LORD is One.'

The Hebrew word *echad* implies diversity existing in unity. God has distinct aspects of his being that come together in harmony. That is how he presents himself to us. The core message of the *Shema* is that we are called to respond to him by loving him with our whole being and acknowledging him as the centre of every area of our lives. Not only does Shalom cover these four areas but you can be in poverty in all four areas too.

God's holistic way of dealing with us is further under-lined in Jesus' mission statement, recorded for us in Luke 4:18–19:

> *The Spirit of the Lord is on me,*
> *   because he has anointed me*
> *   to proclaim good news to the poor.*
> *He has sent me to proclaim freedom for the prisoners*
> *   and recovery of sight for the blind,*
> *to set the oppressed free,*
> *   to proclaim the year of the Lord's favour.*
> (NIV)

To be poor means to be impoverished or lacking, which Jesus expands on after the word 'poor'. A more literal reading of these verses is, *'He has anointed me to proclaim good news to the poor. He has sent me to proclaim freedom for the [poor] prisoners and recovery of sight to the [poor] blind, to set the [poor] oppressed free . . .'*

God is addressing the multi-faceted problem of poverty and countering it with his multi-faceted blessing of prosperity. If you try to remove the issue of money from God's message of prosperity, then you might as well remove divine healing too, whether physical or emotional. In fact, you can't – they are intertwined aspects of God's whole plan for our lives.

Not only are there four areas to prosper in but four areas to be in poverty. This is why Jesus asked, 'What does it profit you to gain the whole world but lose your soul?' He is not saying that prospering will cause you to lose your soul. Instead, he is speaking of the blessing of God covering all four areas.

You begin to truly prosper when you allow God to position himself at the very centre of your life so that his presence permeates every area. Just as God is 'one', he wants you to surrender your life to him as 'one' – the whole of your life, every area. The degree to which you surrender control to him affects the release of his blessing into the whole of your life. The journey to becoming truly prosperous begins when you grasp this concept and begin to live it.

Gary Clarke, Lead Pastor of Hillsong Church, London, says, 'The abandonment of self-purpose and surrendering to God's purpose, no matter what it is in our lives, means changing from our desires to his desires as our focus. We need to learn how, instead of our old nature, to develop our new nature.'

When it comes to the issue of money, I believe that most people need to re-evaluate where their focus lies. To that end I want to challenge some of the commonly held, but erroneous, beliefs that many people hold on to. My hope is that like the Berean Jews mentioned in Acts, who *'received the message with great eagerness and examined the Scriptures every day to see if what Paul said was true'* (Acts 17:11, NIV), you will remain open to consider what I am saying and then search the Bible to uncover these truths for yourself.

I find many Christians are afraid to look into money because it can be dangerous or evil. If all the good people decide to avoid prospering financially, then the only people left with money are all the bad people! Let's not be like an ostrich with its head in the sand. When we are aware of the potential pitfalls in any area of our life, we can learn to avoid them.

As a young Jewish boy I came to trust in *Yeshua* as Messiah. God then took me on a journey to enable me to see the real meaning of wealth and prosperity – prosperity with a purpose; to become a blessing to others as well as enjoying God's unmerited grace and favour myself.

One of my favourite psalms says,

How can a young man cleanse his way?
By taking heed according to your word.
With my whole heart I have sought you;
Oh, let me not wander from your commandments!
Your word I have hidden in my heart,
That I might not sin against you.
(Psalm 119:9–11)

It is another passage that calls us to a place of whole-hearted surrender. I refer to it often to remind myself that God is first in every single area of my life. When I came to Christ my life was messed up; having tried in vain to improve my situation I had come to the end of myself. It was time to turn control over to God. He taught me that as I applied this principle to my life and put him in the driving seat, my life would be blessed and I would prosper.

As I began applying these principles and began to prosper, my Jewish relatives could not help but notice. Often when a Jewish person commits their life to following Christ they are ostracised by their family, but my family were just pleased to see me turn my life around, as I left the drug culture of the streets behind me. They were both amazed and proud to see me becoming successful in business and were curious to find out the secret to my success.

Every time someone asked me about it, I would respond by saying, 'The CEO of my company is Jewish. His name is *Yeshua Ha-Mashiach* – Jesus the Messiah.'

In the early years of going on this journey of financial freedom I realised pretty quickly that my brains alone would not get me there. I needed to do finance God's way. To distinguish between the 'world's way' or 'God's way', I had to be prepared to listen to God's Word and seek his peace (*shalom*). Was I really after the truth, no matter how uncomfortable to the flesh, or was I only looking for the answer I wanted to hear?

I decided to seriously study the Word and stay away from my own casual thoughts. The first step was to ask myself, how does God think about prosperity? It was in the Bible; I just had to 'dig it out'.

Isaiah 55:8–9 says,

'For my thoughts are not your thoughts,
Nor are your ways my ways,' says the LORD.
'For as the heavens are higher than the earth,
So are my ways higher than your ways,
and my thoughts than your thoughts.'

I was fortunate enough to grasp this truth early on and say to God, 'Okay, Lord, I realise that I don't think like you, so please teach me . . .' I wanted to align my thinking with his and rather than rationalising or applying human wisdom to situations, to apply godly wisdom. I searched the Scriptures in order to absorb as much truth as I could and I sought to live constantly in a place of surrender.

The result was that God ran my life so much better than I ever could on my own. Starting to grasp stewardship is an exciting thing. The biblical approach to finance is part of the kingdom of God. Everything seems to be upside down; the roots are in heaven.

It's wonderful to achieve financial freedom, but what greater purpose does our abundance serve? The day I surrendered and dedicated my earthly possessions to God, I transferred my ownership to God and then I became a steward. I felt at peace knowing I was the co-pilot and he is the pilot.

People often tell me that they don't believe in the 'prosperity message'. I know exactly what they mean, and why they feel so strongly about it. Over the years, certain Bible teachers have taken the essence of God's truth regarding prosperity and focused only on the money aspect. By so doing, they have moved money from its proper context, God's holistic view of our overall wellbeing.

Any truth in the Bible can be taken to an unhelpful extreme, at which point it becomes contaminated and distorted by human wisdom. The topic of money has been abused more than most. It has left people with misgivings about those who speak about money. Deep down, people suspect that Bible teachers who speak a lot about money do so because they want theirs!

We all know that we can be doing really well in one area

of our life, but at the same time be bankrupt in another. Creative people, such as professional singers for instance, will often become very successful by using their gift. But we are all familiar with media reports on the casualties of the music business – people whose private lives are in turmoil, despite their success.

People mistakenly think that success in one area of their life will spread to every part, but it does not. A great creative gift has to be supported by great character; otherwise somewhere along the line there will be trouble. Hard work and dedication help to get you to the top but character is what keeps you there.

Spiritually, we may think we are doing great and yet be locking God out of our financial life. Many people do this. It is an unsustainable position and prevents the flow of God's blessing in our life – just as much as a more obvious problem will, like harbouring unforgiveness or bitterness.

Let's go back to Deuteronomy and the Shema.

Deuteronomy 6:5 (NIV) says,

Love the LORD your God with all your heart and with all your soul and with all your strength.

The word 'strength' in Hebrew is *medocha* which means money! So this really should read, 'Love the Lord your God with all your money.'

There is a huge difference between stewardship and ownership. How we view our belongings and our finances is linked to how much we have stepped into a position of surrender to God. If I have surrendered my possessions and finances to him, then I am no longer the owner of those things, just their steward. I no longer strive between serving

God or mammon (the god of money) because I gave all of my mammon to God.

Now I just serve God. I don't own anything anymore – it all belongs to God. It has been said that the beginning of your life is your death. Similarly, the first step on the road to financial freedom is the laying down of all our worth and turning it over to God. Once we do that, we have taken an important step forward.

God's desire to prosper us

What God wants is a takeover, not a makeover!

A friend once said to me, 'Jeff, I don't know if it's really God's will to bless me financially.' I responded, 'On the contrary, it is *absolutely* God's will to bless you financially, because he has said he wants to bless the *whole* of your life.'

Why did my friend assume that God did not want to prosper him financially? Like so many people he had disconnected the issue of money from the rest of his life, particularly his spiritual life. He didn't understand that God deals with us holistically, that he desires to be present at the centre of our finances as well as everything else.

My friend's expectation was therefore that God was committed to blessing him spiritually, but not financially. Yet financial blessing is simply one facet of living under the favour of God in every area of your life.

The *Shalom* of God

When I speak about the topic of finance at churches and conferences, I generally show people this simple diagram as it illustrates how God views our life. It shows the four main areas each of our lives comprise – our spiritual life, relationships, health and finances – and places God at the centre.

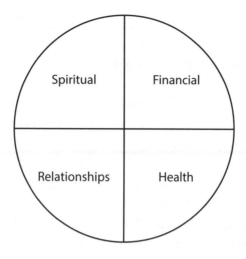

These four components make up the fabric of our lives. Every single day we live, we are functioning in these four zones, even though at any given point our focus may be more on one area than another. The degree to which we succeed in any and all of these areas is the degree to which we surrender them to God's control.

God is interested in blessing each of these areas of your life. You may be familiar with the Hebrew word *shalom*. Most people understand it to mean 'peace'. It does mean that, but it means much more besides. When the Apostle Paul writes that he wants the peace of God to dwell richly in our hearts it conveys a meaning much deeper than most western readers would immediately appreciate.

Shalom means wholeness, wellness, wellbeing, happiness, favour, completeness, security, prosperity, victory, contentment and tranquillity. The concept of *shalom* encompasses the spiritual, physical, emotional, mental, and relational aspects of our lives along with our work and our health. The fact that it occurs almost 500 times in Scripture emphasises its importance.

It is the conclusion to Aaron's great priestly blessing of Numbers 6:26: *'The LORD lift up his countenance upon you, and give you peace [shalom].'* Jesus said *'Peace, be still,'* and *'My peace I give to you.'*

The root of *shalom* means 'to restore' in the sense of replacing or providing what is needed, to make someone or something whole and complete.

In John chapter 5 we read the story of Jesus visiting the pool at Bethesda – a place where, it was rumoured, sick people occasionally got healed by some form of angelic intervention. Jesus encountered a man there who had been sick for thirty-eight years. Verse 6 says that, *'When Jesus saw him lying there, and knew that he had already been in that condition for a long time, he said to him, "Do you want to be made well?"'*

It is interesting that Jesus did not say to the man, 'You've been sick for a long time – do you want to be healed?' In recounting the event, John uses the Greek word *genesthai*, which our modern translations render 'made'. It is the word from which we derive the English word 'genesis' and means 'to be generated' or 'to come into existence'. Then John uses the word *hugies*, which is translated 'well' but its fuller meaning is 'healthy, sound and whole'.

So while Jesus acknowledges that the man has serious health issues, he chooses not to focus solely on his sickness. Rather he asks the man, 'Do you want to become a whole person?' Jesus wants to see the man restored to a state of wholeness and completeness, so that not just his health but his whole life is brought under the Shalom of God.

The bottom line is: God is committed to our wholeness; to bring us to completeness in every area of our lives.

Two ways to get wealth

When we compartmentalise our lives and attempt to deal with the issues of life in isolation from one another, we are bound for trouble and a lack of harmony and peace. Finance is probably the area that people most wrestle with giving over to God. The danger of getting money is that it enables us to be the kind of person we really wanted to be.

Proverbs 11:28 (NIV) tells us what happens when we ignore God and focus only on the acquisition of wealth:

Those who trust in their riches will fall,
but the righteous will thrive like a green leaf.

Many people misinterpret this verse, so it is worthy of closer examination. It is tempting to assume that the person trusting in riches must be an unbeliever and the righteous person must be a believer; i.e. the righteous believer, who is not enticed by material things, will flourish.

More than a few people have used this verse to inform me that the acquisition of wealth would eventually draw me away from God and cause me to stop trusting in him. That's not what this scripture is saying. It is not targeting wealth in a negative sense. Yes, it is a clear warning to put our trust in God as Lord of our life and not other things – for example, material wealth. Trusting in riches is what is highlighted as dangerous. You can be rich and still trust God with all your heart – especially if you view wealth in its proper, biblical context.

The truth is, we need to avoid the misuse of money if we don't want to fail, just as we need to avoid the misuse of food if we don't want to be overweight. Any area of our life that is not submitted to God is out of alignment with him, and will prevent life from functioning well. Anything that we exalt above God becomes idol worship.

Proverbs 10:22 and 1 Timothy 6:9 provide a good contrast of the way in which people think about and pursue wealth:

The blessing of the LORD makes one rich,
and he adds no sorrow with it.

But those who desire to be rich fall into temptation and a snare,
and into many foolish and harmful lusts which drown men in
destruction and perdition.

In simple terms, there are two ways to get rich: the biblical way and the worldly way. In its right context, wealth can be an immense blessing, which we will look at more closely in a later chapter. Taken out of context, we may enjoy the acquisition of wealth and all it brings for a time, but ultimately it will not contribute to our wholeness. It can simply be a trap, slowly but surely enticing us into areas where we never wanted to go.

I have found that money makes good people better and bad people worse! Money reveals the real you and your true heart. Our focus must be upon God and the pursuit of his presence. Placing him at the centre of our lives means that his blessing will flow freely in our lives and he will make us 'rich' in every area.

Character helps us have the right attitude

If we want to make sure that we retain a right attitude towards money (and our spiritual life, health and relationships), then we need to allow God to work on our character. It has been said that the Christian life is more about what happens during our life journey than it is about simply reaching our destination.

Much has been written about how God works to shape our character through the people, events and circumstances in our lives. I won't explore that in detail here, but I do want to emphasise one thing. Perhaps the greatest character attribute we can develop that will help us to handle our finances well is thankfulness. Being mindful of what God has given us and expressing genuine gratitude for it is a valuable asset. When you live with a grateful heart and put God first in your finances it keeps your ego in check, for you realise it was God's blessings and not you alone.

Deuteronomy 8:10 says,

When you have eaten and are full, then you shall bless the LORD your God for the good land which he has given you.

I like to be a bit provocative and ask people if they say grace before or after a meal. Most Christians say it beforehand, but the Bible clearly says we should give thanks after we have eaten. It makes sense to me.

God instructed his people to give thanks for his provision, because when we take for granted what we have, an ungrateful spirit can set in. People will make all kinds of promises to God when they are in need, but will become ambivalent when all their needs are being met. The key is to remain grateful *after* your need has been met.

Deuteronomy 8:11–15 continues,

Beware that you do not forget the LORD your God by not keeping his commandments, his judgments, and his statutes which I command you today, lest – when you have eaten and are full, and have built beautiful houses and dwell in them . . . you forget the LORD your God who brought you out of the land of Egypt, from the house of bondage . . .

I call this spiritual amnesia! We are most likely to misuse money when we forget the one who has provided us with it. Retaining a thankful heart is the best way of remembering that our riches come from God. Never become complacent or lazy in your attitude, but be grateful for the goodness of God in your life.

A continual heart of gratitude to God ensures a continual flow of God's blessings. Money provides solutions and has the power to change situations, to make a big difference in our choices. God desires us to have financial peace along with the other three areas of our lives. This is the true peace and shalom of God.

In summary, God wants a *takeover* in your life, not a *makeover*.

Chapter 3

A Fresh Perspective on Money and Stewardship

Often in life we do things because we have always done them that way; it's called habit or tradition. We believe things because we have been told them, often without checking out their veracity for ourselves.

There is a story of a newly married woman who cooked a nice dinner of roast ham for her husband one night. He asked her why she had cut it into two pieces before putting it in the oven and she said, surprised, that it was the way her mother always did it. Then the young woman checked out the cooking method with her mother who said, 'Oh – I only did that because my pan was too small to fit the whole ham!' The daughter assumed it had to be done a particular way without ever questioning why.

This is also true when it comes to our finances. People will believe things they have been told, just because they sound like they *ought to be* true. This is one of the reasons why people hold on to distorted views of money and wealth. Statements like:

- Money is the root of all evil.
- You can't be rich and happy.
- Jesus was poor, so you should be too.
- Money will corrupt you, so stay away from it.
- Only greedy people become wealthy.

These sayings lack a biblical foundation. Many of them are passed on from generation to generation and eventually they become like concrete: all mixed up and set!

In this chapter let us look at some of Jesus' teachings on finance that address how people view money. We will see how he sought to change their thinking about finance from being self-focused to God-focused. It is interesting that the majority of Jesus' parables relate to money!

The parable of the unjust steward
This unconventional parable is notable because it is one of only a few parables in which Jesus uses a story about an unrighteous person to illustrate a point about righteousness. Luke 16:1–13 records it:

In the story, a rich man is about to fire his steward for mismanagement of his master's resources. A great deal of trust had been placed in the steward, as he had complete authority to conduct his master's business affairs. He was being fired for bad management, not necessarily fraudulent dealing, though he was fundamentally dishonest.

Realising he would shortly be out of work, the steward rushed to complete a few final deals, collecting a significant amount of money owed to the business by reducing the debts in return for swift payment. When the master discovered what he had done, instead of being furious, he actually commended the steward for his business acumen and shrewd operating.

Jesus was speaking to his disciples and some Pharisees. The disciples came from a variety of social backgrounds. Some were fishermen, entrepreneurs, and one a tax collector. But all Jesus' listeners would have been familiar with financial stewards, business debts and the often punitive, interest-laden repayments that were demanded.

Most listeners would have expected the master in the story to have been incensed by his steward's corrupt behaviour, but Jesus deliberately shocked his audience by saying that, on the contrary, the master commended the steward for his sharp practice. It is important to remember here that it is not Jesus who is commending the man for his actions, just the boss in the story!

Jesus is illustrating for us the relationship between the rich master and his steward. The steward had handled his master's resources carelessly and was now being threatened with having everything stripped away from him. The steward then came up with a scheme to get himself out of trouble. He was quite creative!

The likely setting for this tale, in agricultural Israel, is that of a large estate divided into smaller sections and rented out to individuals. The steward's job was to manage the tenants and collect the rent. He had let the debts mount up and now the master was owed a great deal of money. Acting as if he has not been fired, the steward rushed around the tenants, offered to reduce the amount of their debts if they pay up immediately, and got them to sign on the dotted line.

The steward somehow created a win-win scenario from one of certain doom. The tenants were of course happy with him (and by extension, his master) for being so generous. His master was pleased with him because all the tenants were happy and he had received a very large boost to his cash flow overnight. The steward was happy because, rather than kicking him out, his master acknowledged his business acumen and tenacity. What a turnaround!

Jesus labels the focus of this business transaction as 'unrighteous mammon'. There was shrewdness to the deal as well as an element of ruthlessness. Yet Jesus comments that, often, the children of the world are wiser when it comes to handling finances than the children of light, a very sad commentary on believers. Then he cuts to the heart of his message:

He who is faithful in what is least [money] is faithful also in much; and he who is unjust in what is least [money] is unjust also in much. Therefore if you have not been faithful in the unrighteous mammon [money], who will commit to your trust the true riches? And if you have not been faithful in what is another man's, who will give you what is your own? No servant can serve two masters; for either he will hate the one and love the other, or else he will be loyal to the one and despise the other. You cannot serve God and mammon.
(Luke 16:10–13)

Two overarching principles that Jesus brings into sharp focus for us are:

1. The quality of our stewardship.
2. The focus of our serving.

When we take the correct biblical view that all we have actually belongs to God, it should change the way we steward those resources. If we truly believe that it is not *our money*, but *God's money*, then that will affect how we administrate our finances. We are not owners, we are stewards. God is the owner; we get to manage his belongings.

It is easy for God to get money to you, but can he get it through you?

So, the first challenge Jesus has for us is: *What kind of steward are you?* Are you positioning yourself as a trustworthy person that God can use to channel his resources through? When you get money in its proper place, the other three areas of our lives fall into place, with the Shalom of God covering us. This is true riches.

Then Jesus shows us the method: we become trustworthy stewards by beginning with a little and handling it faithfully. *'He who is faithful in what is least is faithful also in much . . .'* The journey to being entrusted with true riches is a journey of character development. Though we only have a little, if we handle it with integrity and wisdom, then God will entrust us with more. He releases more to us in line with the growth of our character and, therefore, our ability to handle it.

God is not going to make you wealthy overnight if he knows you don't have the maturity or character to sustain it. He cares more about who you are becoming than about what you have. Your net worth will gradually grow as your self-worth and overall wealth grows.

The second challenge Jesus has for us is: *Who are you serving?* It is a reminder not to focus on the resources God allows us to steward on his behalf but, instead, to keep our eyes fixed on him. Our focus must always be on the Giver, not the gift.

Most people worry about money. They worry about not having enough – not enough to pay the bills, not enough to afford that thing they want, not enough to afford a holiday. And what if something unexpected happens? How are they going to pay for that?

In short, the focus is all on the money. Jesus wants us to

stop looking at the money and look at God. First, we remember it is all his – we are just looking after it. Second, we do not get caught up with it – we keep our focus on our heavenly Father who has promised to provide for us. We shift from trusting in money to trusting in God. We use wisdom in handling money but we hold it with a loose grip.

If our priorities lie in the wrong place, then we need to shift our focus.

The rich young ruler

Chapter 19 of Matthew records a fascinating and illuminating meeting that Jesus had with a wealthy young man. Afterwards, he had a discussion with his disciples about money and material possessions, which yields further important principles for us.

In Matthew 19:16–22 we read first about the encounter itself:

Now behold, one came and said to him, 'Good teacher, what good thing shall I do that I may have eternal life?' So he said to him, 'Why do you call me good? No one is good but one, that is, God. But if you want to enter into life, keep the commandments.' He said to him, 'Which ones?' Jesus said, 'You shall not murder,' 'You shall not commit adultery,' 'You shall not steal,' 'You shall not bear false witness,' 'Honour your father and your mother,' and, 'You shall love your neighbour as yourself.'

The young man said to him, 'All these things I have kept from my youth. What do I still lack?' Jesus said to him, 'If you want to be perfect, go, sell what you have and give to the poor, and you will have treasure in heaven; and come, follow me.' But when the young man heard that saying, he went away sorrowful, for he had great possessions.

Before looking at what Jesus has to say about this, it is worth pausing to look at the young man. Luke tells us that he was young, wealthy and a ruler (possibly a magistrate; see Luke 18:18). Yet despite all he had achieved at a young age, he recognised Jesus' wisdom as a teacher and greatly respected him. Mark's account describes him running up to Jesus and kneeling before him. He demonstrated a willingness to learn from the Master, identifying Jesus as 'Good Teacher' (though Jesus immediately directs his focus to God).

We also learn that the young man believed in eternal life and wanted to make sure he attained it – unusual given both his wealth and his age. He had settled in his mind that, as one commentator put it, 'eternal life is not a game of chance or blind fate.' He had also recognised in Jesus someone who could point him in the right direction. Could Jesus be the mentor he needed to take him to a new level in his life?

Next we see Jesus respond to the young man's question regarding the commandments. 'If you want to enter life,' he said, 'then keep the commandments.' Jesus went on to list just six out of the Ten Commandments. I don't know about you, but I have never heard about Moses and the Six Commandments. Why did Jesus not recite all ten?

Jesus was preparing to touch on a sensitive area – that of the young man's wealth and how he viewed it. He made no mention of the commandments regarding covetousness or idolatry – the sin of desiring that which belongs to someone else, and the sin of elevating something above our love for God. Maybe these two things were the real issues for this man? But Jesus chose not to focus on them. Instead he showed his compassion for the man and tried to draw him in, put him on the correct path to have prosperity in all areas of his life.

Maybe with a touch of youthful arrogance, the man claimed that he had kept all of these commandments since he was young. So what else would he need to do? This is when Jesus touched on the raw nerve, which happens to be his wallet. *'If you want to be perfect, [be complete, have shalom] go, sell what you have and **give to the poor**, and you will have treasure in heaven; and come, follow me.'*

Let us pause here for a moment. It is easy to misinterpret what is being said. People are fond of saying that Jesus taught we have to give away all our money to the poor. No, he told the young man to 'sell what you have' and **give to the poor**. It is an important distinction.

Nowhere in Scripture are we instructed to give away every single thing that we have. This would be a violation of a larger biblical principle. God instructed the nation of Israel never to eat their seed corn. They needed it to plant for next year's harvest. Every 'seed' that God places in our hands has the potential to either be eaten or planted. If you eat all the seed corn then you have nothing left to plant and, pretty soon, your resources will be decimated.

Instead, Jesus instructed the young man to be generous with the wealth he had been blessed with and, at the same time, tried to help him to see the source of that blessing as God himself. 'If you use that wealth correctly,' Jesus said, 'then you'll discover the source of true riches.'

Jesus was speaking about stewardship again. The truth he wanted to impart to the young man is about recognising the source of our wealth and then stewarding it in a way that is pleasing to God. If he took Jesus' advice, the young man would be richly blessed.

Anyone who really understood Jewish teaching would have known this proverb:

He who has pity on the poor lends to the LORD,
And he will pay back what he has given.
(Proverbs 19:17)

The young man found the challenge too great and the step of faith too constraining. Whether he inherited wealth or made it as an entrepreneur he found it impossible to grasp Jesus' upside-down economics. How can we become wealthy by giving some of our wealth away? It makes no sense when examined through the filter of earthly wisdom.

Yet it makes perfect sense when viewed through the filter of godly wisdom and biblical economics. The problem with money is that it really exposes your heart. I can look at your chequebook or bank statement and tell where your priorities are. This young man could not let go of ownership and release it all to God.

Following this incident, Jesus told his disciples how hard it is for rich people to enter the kingdom of God.

Then Jesus said to his disciples, 'Assuredly I say to you that it is hard for a rich man to enter the kingdom of heaven. And again I say to you, it is easier for a camel to go through the eye of a needle than for a rich man to enter the kingdom of God.'
(Matthew 19:23–24)

Jesus' point was not that we need to forsake wealth in order to enter the kingdom of God. Not at all, for once again this would contradict the greater principle of God's message of blessing and prosperity.

Jesus was making an entirely different point and using hyperbole to underline it, just as he did when he spoke about removing the plank from our own eye before attending to the speck of dust in someone else's. On that occasion, he wasn't speaking about literal planks and dust – he was using exaggeration to make a point. The disciples were puzzled by Jesus' words about possessing wealth and entering the kingdom, so they responded accordingly:

When his disciples heard it, they were greatly astonished, saying, 'Who then can be saved?'
(verse 25)

It is interesting to note that these are not the words of the financially destitute. If the disciples themselves were paupers, why would they have responded in this way? As Jews they understood the Abrahamic blessing and that, if they followed God's covenant, they would prosper in every area of their lives and possess financial wealth. They understood the promise in Deuteronomy 8:18 that God gave them power to get wealth. Their biblical understanding was being challenged.

Jesus cut to the heart of the matter:

Jesus looked at them and said to them, 'With men this is impossible, but with God all things are possible.'
(verse 26)

Another way of saying this is that Jesus looked at them and said, 'With men [by ourselves] this is impossible, but with God [as the centre of our lives] all things are possible.'

My interpretation is: We human beings left to ourselves and our own fallen nature and selfish ways will go astray. But with God involved in the core and centre of our lives, all things are possible. When our entire focus is money, it is impossible to be a kingdom person. When our focus and central theme is God, all things are possible.

Jesus was saying that if you are focused on your wealth as your source then you will find it difficult to connect with God. God refuses to play second fiddle to your finances or anything else. He wants your full attention, devotion and surrender.

Many people prioritise their financial affairs above their relationship with God, viewing them as separate concerns. But if that equation is turned on its head, Jesus says, then God can release a miracle for you. If God is at the centre of your life, then your riches will be in their correct place – subservient to the Father. Your money becomes his money, entrusted to you. You become a steward and no longer the owner.

You then become directed in your finances by the Holy Spirit and God's Word, which will never contradict each other. This is why tithing proves that God is of first importance, because the first thing you do with money is to put God first.

Not quite getting the full implication of Jesus' truth, Peter protested:

'See, we have left all and followed you. Therefore what shall we have?'
(verse 27)

Jesus responded by pointing Peter towards the bigger picture – the reward that awaits all who faithfully serve God and exalt him as the pivotal point of their lives.

Jesus said to them, 'Assuredly I say to you . . . everyone who has left houses or brothers or sisters or father or mother or wife or children or lands, for my name's sake, shall receive a hundred-fold, and inherit eternal life.'
(verses 28–29)

'Left houses' or 'forsaken' simply means that you have not exalted your house or family or anything else above God. It does not mean that you have literally given away your house and lands or rejected your family. *Anything you put before God or exalt above God becomes 'idol worship'.*

Whatever we sacrifice in surrender to God – whether finances or relationships or anything else – he will return in blessing according to a measure far greater than we can imagine. We need to trust him in all areas of our life. When God is the centre of our relationships, health, spiritual and financial life, his shalom covers us and we then have a peace that rests on everything. We are promised a 'hundredfold' and eternal life. Hundredfold means now, and eternal life means later.

Let's take our attention off money, and focus on making him our first love.

CHAPTER 4

A Fresh Perspective on Tithing and Giving

Finance in our hands always has a deeper potential purpose than just meeting our own needs. The most amazing benefit of putting God at the very centre of our lives is that, over time, he gradually changes us to become more and more like him. The more we surrender to him, the more he is able to shape our character. The more he shapes our character, the more the character of Jesus is visible to others through our lives.

One thing that is clear about the character of God is that he is an incredible giver. He gives freely, generously, and lavishly, and holds nothing back. It is said that in life you are either a giver or a taker. If God has control of your life then you will be a giver, just as he is – or at least you'll be somewhere along the journey to becoming one.

God wants us to learn how to live out of his abundance. He wants us to give freely with no thought of reward. We share out of our love for God, not out of religious guilt.

Giving brings God a great deal of pleasure. He gives in abundance, without measure, and desires that same attitude to characterise the lives of his children. No child of God should ever be satisfied with living hand-to-mouth, because this is not what God desires for you.

Abundance does not flow out of poverty. God wants to pour abundance into our lives and have us pour it out onto others. Then our giving will not be cold or mechanical, something we do because it is demanded of us. Rather it will be an expression of gratitude to the one who meets all our needs, and who blesses and prospers us.

This is the heart behind the biblical principle of giving. It is important to understand this as we turn to look at perhaps the most controversial aspect of giving. I hope you will allow me to tell it like it is, and not dance around some issues on money. I am not being judgmental, but I am going to 'shoot you straight'.

The principle of tithing

Tithing is a hotly debated topic in the Church and there are various conflicting teachings on it currently in circulation. Personally, I believe we can be very clear on the principle and practice of tithing, as long as we understand its place in the larger framework of God's heart for giving. Once again, we need to understand this issue in a holistic sense and not try to examine it in isolation.

Perhaps the most common arguments objecting to tithing are as follows:

1. *'Tithing was an Old Testament practice, part of the Old Covenant. It was therefore superseded by Christ's new covenant.'*
   Proponents of this view believe that tithing has been replaced by the less formal arrangement of 'giving' by

which they mean being generous on occasion and giving money away in unspecified amounts as appropriate.

2. *'Tithing was a system that related to the agricultural community of its day. It is no longer relevant to modern society.'* Proponents of this view claim that tithing was culturally relevant in its context, but since we live in an entirely different culture/context now, it no longer applies.

Let us first establish that tithing is a condition of the heart, not a money issue. It shows your surrender in the area of finance. I tithe because I believe that the teaching of Scripture supports it, so I want to respond to these objections in two ways:

Firstly, I believe that the overarching principle of the tithe is timeless in God's Word. Through Scripture, whenever we read about the tithe we are told that it is something holy and set apart for God. Look, for instance at Leviticus 27:30:

And all the tithe of the land, whether of the seed of the land or of the fruit of the tree, is the LORD's. It is holy to the LORD.

But the principle goes back much further than this. We see in Genesis 2:16 that God gives Adam and Eve free reign of his garden, except for the tree of the knowledge of good and evil. This tree was like a tithe. It was holy and set apart for God. It was not to be touched by anyone else. It was effectively God's 10% of the whole that, though he owned everything, he specially identified as belonging exclusively to him.

By eating the fruit of that tree, Adam and Eve violated the principle of the tithe. It's called covetousness. Covetousness is desiring something that is not *yours*. They wanted the part that was reserved by God, as well as all the rest. As a result they ended up living under a curse. Here is the principle: if you sow a seed, you will reap a harvest – either for good or bad.

Secondly, it's not the outward form or *expression* of the practice that is the most important, but the *heart* of it. Many of the practices of the Old Testament foreshadowed or pointed towards greater spiritual truths. Certain practices may have been done away with over the centuries, but the spiritual principles they pointed to remain.

In Christ, the Law was fulfilled, but he didn't simply scrap the spiritual principles of the Old Covenant. Rather, he took them further and showed us how these principles operate within the setting of grace. Jesus never abolished the former principles, instead he transcended them.

Those who believe in Christ are no longer under the Law, but under grace. The Ten Commandments were under the law, but that doesn't mean it is now okay to murder and violate all the other commandments! God still wishes for us to treat one another with dignity and to have guidelines for living. Did God's concept of morality change when Jesus died on Calvary? Here are the Ten Commandments:

1. You shall have no other gods before me or besides me.
2. You shall not make yourself any graven image.
3. You shall not take the Lord's name in vain.
4. Remember the Sabbath day to keep it holy.
5. Honour your father and mother.
6. You shall not commit murder.
7. You shall not commit adultery.
8. You shall not steal.
9. You shall not witness falsely against your neighbour.
10. You shall not covet your neighbour's house, wife or possessions.

Which ones are we supposed not to keep? We get our righteousness by serving God, not the law, but in serving God, these Ten Commandments will become our moral compass.

But the purpose of grace is to empower us to live the way God wants us to. Romans 8:4 tells us that Jesus came so that the righteous requirement of the law might be fully met in us, not so that we could altogether dismiss it. For this reason, I don't think that cultural relevance has anything to do with the practice of tithing.

The principle of recognising that all we have belongs to God, and the setting apart of a small part of that in recognition of the fact, remains. But now we view tithing not as a requirement of the law, but as an act of thanksgiving for God's amazing grace. You don't have to tithe, you are allowed to tithe! It's a privilege, not an obligation.

Jesus condemned the Pharisees for missing the heart principle of tithing. They were good practitioners of religion and they tithed to the penny, but they missed the whole point of the exercise.

> *'Woe to you, scribes and Pharisees, hypocrites! For you pay tithe of mint and anise and cumin, and have neglected the weightier matters of the law: justice and mercy and faith. These you ought to have done, without leaving the others undone.'*
> (Matthew 23:23)

Notice that Jesus doesn't say, 'You shouldn't have bothered about tithing when there are bigger matters to consider . . .' He tells them that they were right to offer their tithe to God, but they were doing it for the wrong reasons. Tithing is a validation of my love for God, not my fear of him.

In Mark 12:42–44, Jesus comments on a poor widow who brought her offering into the temple treasury.

Then one poor widow came and threw in two mites . . . So he called his disciples to himself and said to them, 'Assuredly, I say to you that this poor widow has put in more than all those who have given to the treasury; for they all put in out of their abundance, but she out of her poverty put in all that she had, her whole livelihood.'

Again Jesus focused on the heart of the giver. Here was a lady who understood the principle of being a giver. The amount of money was irrelevant, in one sense, because she was simply practicing what she knew to be right, despite the little she had.

Many people will say that they would tithe if they could afford to. This lady clearly felt that she couldn't afford *not* to tithe. The amount you give does not indicate your value to God. It is interesting that we are not instructed to give a certain monetary figure, but a percentage. That way everyone gives according to their means. God asks us all for equal sacrifice not equal giving.

Whenever I speak on this topic, I like to demonstrate visually what happens when we tithe. I hold up a loaf of bread and then break off roughly 10% of it. The loaf represents our income and we 'break off' a tenth of it and give it back to God. What happens next is a miracle. Somehow, God covers and causes the 90% we have left to go further than the 100% would have, had we held onto it. This is called the miracle of Malachi.

'Bring all the tithes into the storehouse,
That there may be food in my house,

And try me now in this,'
Says the LORD *of hosts,*
'If I will not open for you the windows of heaven
And pour out for you such blessing
That there will not be room enough to receive it.'
(Malachi 3:10)

These words are at the heart of the debate about whether or not the principle of tithing was carried over into the New Covenant. I believe it was. Nothing Jesus taught contradicts that belief. In fact I cannot find one scripture where Jesus or any other writer in the Bible says not to tithe.

My friend Rabbi Daniel Lapin taught me that the actual Hebrew translation is literally 'tithe, so that you may become wealthy'. Here is what he had to say on the subject of tithing:

We tithe primarily because God tells us to do so. However, His wisdom is revealed in the numerous benefits that come from tithing such as the fact that He created us to feel uplifted by the act of giving. Numerous studies such as that by University of British Columbia psychologist Elizabeth Dunn and many others proves that giving makes us happier people. Second, by the mysterious mechanics I describe in *Thou Shall Prosper*, philanthropy and giving opens up the conduits of revenue for the giver.

In the Lord's language, Hebrew, the word for Tithe comprises the three letters AYIN–SHIN–REISH which happen to be exactly the word that also spells wealth. In Hebrew, the rule is that any two words that are spelled the same are linked and sure enough, ancient Jewish wisdom emphasizes the connection with the words – Tithe so that you may prosper/become wealthy.
(Rabbi Daniel Lapin)

In Malachi 3:6 the scripture says *'I am the* LORD, *I do not change.'* God's values, morals and character are the same today as they were when he created heaven and earth. One thing God does not do is change. Why? Because he is God! God does not grow better with age. Why? Because he is God.

I have heard people say, 'I don't tithe so, are you saying I'm cursed?' No, if you're not a tither you are not cursed – you are just not blessed to the degree you could be. What's the difference?

The difference is that you have effectively ring-fenced your finances from God, as if to say, 'I've got this area covered, God. I don't need your help with it.' God stands back and says, 'Okay then, go for it . . .' It doesn't alter his love for you one iota, but you are stemming the flow of his blessing and going it alone in this area of your life.

You have decided to put 'self' in the middle of the circle when it comes to your finances.

God loves you whether you tithe or not, but there are benefits! I must admit many years ago as a teenager, I started tithing out of fear, not faith. I was taught from Malachi 3:9 that if I did not tithe, a bolt of lightning would strike, or something bad would befall me. I do not believe that now, nor do I believe that is what this scripture means.

Let us explore this deeper. Malachi 3:9 says *'You are cursed with a curse.'* What is this curse?

Genesis 3:17–19 tells of a curse brought by Adam and Eve when they *'ate from the tree about which I commanded you, "You must not eat of it"; Cursed is the ground because of you'* (v. 17 NIV). So by eating of the tree (something holy and set apart by God not to personally consume) they brought about a curse on the earth.

In Malachi 3:9 we find that if we don't put God first we are under the curse of the earth, without God's covering on our crops (our livelihood). In verse 11 we read that our vine will cast off its fruit before it is time; in other words, we will suffer crop failure! By putting God first in our finance and tithing, we ensure God is covering our lives. Either that or we decide to 'self-insure' and do not tithe.

Malachi is the only place in the Bible where God specifically invites us to test him. He says, in effect, 'Go on, I dare you! Test me and see if this doesn't work . . .' He is so committed to blessing and prospering us that he gives us the opportunity to see what will happen if we entrust our money to him.

But again, what he is really after is our heart, not our wallet. Our love for God is authenticated by our deeds and actions, and tithing is one of those actions. Blessings in abundance are always on the other side of obedience. God invites us to participate in a simple act of obedience and in return he offers us wholeness in every area of our life.

We serve a good God. He knows the intentions of our hearts, but our actions speak volumes about what is really in our hearts. Tithing is the manifestation of our hearts.

Proverbs 3:5–8 teaches us to,

Trust in the LORD with all your heart,
and lean not on your own understanding;
in all your ways acknowledge him,
and he shall direct your paths.
Do not be wise in your own eyes;
fear the LORD and depart from evil.
It will be health to your flesh,
and strength to your bones.

We are reminded that often God's methods are alien to us. We cannot compute them with human logic, because they transcend our logic. We just have to trust that he knows what he is doing and what's best for us.

The passage above applies this truth to our finances, as it continues in verses 9–10,

Honour the LORD with your possessions,
and with the first-fruits of all your increase;
so your barns will be filled with plenty,
and your vats will overflow with new wine.

The writer of Proverbs goes on to talk about the benefits of gaining godly wisdom in this area of our life. It results in happiness, with the added sense of being envied by others and having increased influence. It also means a lengthening of our days because God is able to guide us on the right path.

For those who tithe, the peace and abundance that is released by choosing to operate in God's economy is sure to far exceed any financial security that the world has to offer. I have never met anyone who is a tither and a good steward over the other 90%, who is not living a blessed life!

Faithful in small things

In the previous chapter I mentioned that God calls us to be faithful in stewarding little, so that in time he can trust us with much. It helps us to grow steadily into maturity.

This same principle applies to tithing. God requests that we return a small percentage of our income to him and he commits to pouring out an abundant blessing on us. This commitment proves indeed that God is first.

To me, not tithing is like having a spouse and saying, 'I love you, but it is not my responsibility to contribute to the household.' Your words may say 'I love you,' but your actions prove your real intentions and selfishness.

You would never even think of going to a restaurant, ordering, eating and then getting up and walking out without paying the bill. How can I come to the house of God, put my feet under the table, enjoy the message and atmosphere, but refuse to contribute? I love God's house too much to not put him first in my finances.

My very first job was stacking supermarket shelves for $30 a week. Every week I would set aside $3 of that as my tithe and I would usually add a couple of dollars more on top as an offering. Because I established the habit of giving regularly based on these small sums, when I began earning more money I continued the practice.

I think about it in very simple terms: If God cannot trust you with 10% of £30, how can he trust you with 10% of £300, or £3,000 or £30,000 or more? The sums are irrelevant. God just wants to know that he has fully captured your heart. Tithing is not about money, it is about trust – the condition of your heart towards God.

God, our God will take care of the hidden things but the revealed things are our business. It's up to us and our children to attend to all the terms in this revelation.
(Deuteronomy 29:29 THE MESSAGE)

This tells us that God has revealed certain principles to us, but that others are secret. The secret things belong to the Lord, but one thing he has clearly revealed to us is the law of sowing and reaping. The tithe is simply learning to live by faith and trusting God that 90% goes further than 100%!

One of the keys to our life is generosity. Tithes and offerings, and good stewardship of our money, are the password to prosperity.

The principle of sowing seed

When we tithe we are planting a seed, and a seed eventually produces a harvest. God gives us the natural things in the world as examples of how the spiritual things work. As an example, an apple can be eaten but inside there are a number of seeds that can be planted and grown. The interesting thing is that these seeds will produce not one apple, but several trees which may eventually yield thousands of apples. Now the example here illustrates how when we sow in the natural there is a yield. When we sow financially into God's kingdom there is also a yield.

You can never out-give God. What could I possibly give God back for his goodness and mercy shown to me? The only thing I know to give back to God is my life, and this includes my heart, my mind, my soul and my finances. If God shows no boundaries in his love towards us, how can we not reciprocate? The tithe is simply a foundation for giving based on principle and not emotion. It takes faith to plant a seed in the ground and believe that, in due course, it will return a harvest.

This is what our tithe is: a seed, planted in faith. We plant it by giving it to God and then allow him to nurture it and cause it to bloom into harvest. He promises to bless us abundantly. He cannot do that if we do not plant a seed and in order to sow or reap you have to first release!

Jensen Franklin says, 'God expects you to do what you can do, then he will do what you can't do.' You may not have a clue how to create a financial harvest, but you do know how to plant a small seed by way of tithing. When that seed is in God's hands, he can do something amazing with it.

The multi-faceted blessing

In return for our small act of obedience in sowing our tithe,

God responds with a multi-faceted blessing, promising a whole spectrum of benefits.

1. **He opens the windows of heaven** (Malachi 3:10). God begins to open up the resources of heaven over your life. Sometimes this comes in the form of divine connections or favour on your life from others.
2. **He pours out uncontainable blessing** (3:10). God blessed Adam and Eve with fruitfulness, but their disobedience cost them the blessing. God blessed Abraham (Genesis 12) and this blessing has been transmitted to us through Christ (Galatians 3:29). Our obedience to Christ positions us in the full flow of God's blessing.
3. **Our crops will be abundant, but also protected by God** (3:11). God promises that our small investment will be returned in abundance. In addition, he puts his seal of blessing on what we already have, preventing it from being devoured. This could mean anything from protecting our financial investments from going bad to causing our washing machine to last much longer than normal without breaking.

   When we sow in faith, God responds supernaturally! He adds his 'super' to our 'natural'. When you are not tithing, all you have is your 'natural' with no 'super' to go with it! You made the decision to do things your way. God still loves you but you will have isolated this area from his direct covering. You are not in covenant with him in finance. If you are not tithing, do not feel under condemnation. God still loves you, but you just will not be receiving the benefits of tithing. Why should you?
4. **You will be called blessed** (3:12). Those who walk in the blessing of God begin to be noticed by others. When we are in the flow of God's prosperity, this

makes an impression on others. We begin to become influencers.

5. **Your land will be delightful** (3:12). God effectively promises us his peace and joy as we walk in obedience to him. Others will remark on your tranquillity, recession or no recession.

I believe that many Christians fail to make tithing a habit because they see it as something onerous, and they baulk at the idea of a mandatory requirement. In other words, they see it as a tax when, in truth, it is an investment. What is more, it is an investment without risk; an investment that cannot fail. No investment portfolio in the world will ever produce the kind of returns that God offers.

But remember, tithing is not a mechanism we use to twist God's arm to bless us. He wants to bless us and he frequently does bless us, even while we are rebellious towards him in so many other areas of our lives. Rather, tithing is a sign to God that we acknowledge all we have is his. It is a sign of our obedience; a sign of our trust in him.

If you do not do it already, I urge you to give to God. Allow him to soften your heart and express his abundant character through you. Learn to embrace the giving heart of God and to emulate it yourself. Learn to be a giver, rather than just a taker.

Tithing for me sets the bar of consistent giving and this stabilises my life. This unselfish action shows my love for God and his house. Having money carries with it responsibility and a choice to do it God's way.

As I have personally studied what the Bible has to say about money, I have tried to maintain an open heart and mind to God. Other people have brought up some fantastic questions and observations which has made me even more determined to 'search the scriptures' for the truth on the subject of tithes and offerings. I love curious minds and open hearts who truly want to seek out the truth, not just a justification for their position. I have spent hundreds of hours studying this subject and have never found one scripture that says 'do not tithe'.

I do not believe that tithing makes you any more 'righteous' than the person who does not tithe. This 'righteousness' or right standing with God is established when we accept Jesus. I believe in grace, but I also believe in operating by godly principles. Jesus' death on the cross did not do away with God's character or his nature. God is still God.

The real purpose of tithing

Can you be trusted with someone else's possessions? Tithing is not a money issue but a heart issue. It is all about the amount of trust I have and faith in God supplying provision for me. When I tithe this shows that I am putting God before everything else. I am acknowledging what is rightfully his in the first place.

It also shows that my actions speak louder than my words. The act of tithing is the outward acknowledgement that all blessings from God come from him. God operates out of his character, not his feelings, and he expects us to do the same as a sign of our maturity in Christ.

This principle of tithing and offerings is in both the Old and New Testament. The tithe is not mine but God's in the first place. How can God have 'space' to pour us out a blessing if we do not first do our part and return to him what is rightfully his? This is entering into covenant with God.

Is there a difference in tithing and offerings? Definitely yes! I will show you in the next few pages what the differences are.

What is the tithe?

The tithe is always 10% throughout the Scriptures – see Genesis 14:20, and Hebrews 7:2. You cannot tithe more than 10%. Anything you give above this 10% is not a tithe but an offering.

The tithe is a constant 10% and it is a 'trust' relationship with us and God. He trusts us as a steward with his money, so we are simply returning back to God what is rightfully his. Tithing proves to God that we can be trusted with his resources.

Luke 16:12 shows us that if we cannot exert authority (discipline and consistency) over our own finances, we are incapable of exerting authority over others. Tithing shows consistency and faithfulness (Luke 16:10–11). Tithing shows that we are putting God first and not ourselves. The tithe is the Lord's (not ours) – Leviticus 27:30.

Because tithing is a command, observing it is a statement of our obedience to God and not our own way of thinking. Like most things that are godly, tithing goes against the flesh! But it is a key to an 'open heaven' in my life.

Tithing is still in the New Testament. The writer of Hebrews in chapter 7 verse 8 says, *'Here mortal men receive tithes.'* This means here and now! It was understood and ingrained in people's hearts and beliefs.

In Luke 11:42 Jesus does not dismiss tithing, but instead praises it. He rarely taught on it because it was part of his life and everyone else that followed him. Why would he need to address it if they were already doing it?

Tithing was never meant to be a burden but a blessing, a privilege and not an obligation. When we tithe consistently it shows our consistent gratitude to God and acknowledgement of where our resources came from.

The place to give the tithe is determined in the Scriptures – the storehouse is where you get fed. This is the local church. (If you are not getting fed, find a church in which you can get fed and grow.)

What is an offering?

There is no need for me to write to you about this service to the Lord's people. For I know your eagerness to help, and I have been boasting about it to the Macedonians, telling them that since last year you in Achaia were ready to give; and your enthusiasm has stirred most of them to action. But I am sending the brothers in order that our boasting about you in this matter should not prove hollow, but that you may be ready, as I said you would be. For if any Macedonians come with me and find you unprepared, we – not to say anything about you – would be ashamed of having been so confident. So I thought it necessary to urge the brothers to visit you in advance and finish the arrangements for the generous gift you had promised. Then it will be ready as a generous gift, not as one grudgingly given.

Remember this: Whoever sows sparingly will also reap sparingly, and whoever sows generously will also reap generously. Each of you should give what you have decided in your heart to give, not reluctantly or under compulsion, for God loves a cheerful giver. And God is able to bless you abundantly, so that in all things at all times, having all that you need, you will abound in every good work. As it is written:

*'They have freely scattered their gifts to the poor;
    their righteousness endures forever.'*

Now he who supplies seed to the sower and bread for food will also supply and increase your store of seed and will enlarge the harvest of your righteousness. You will be enriched in every way so that you can be generous on every occasion, and through us your generosity will result in thanksgiving to God.

This service that you perform is not only supplying the needs of the Lord's people but is also overflowing in many expressions of thanks to God. Because of the service by which you have proved yourselves, others will praise God for the obedience that accompanies your confession of the gospel of Christ, and for your generosity in sharing with them and with everyone else. And in their prayers for you their hearts will go out to you, because of the surpassing grace God has given you. Thanks be to God for his indescribable gift!

(2 Corinthians 9:1–15 NIV)

So often 2 Corinthians 9:6–7 is quoted as if to say, 'I am just supposed to give out of the goodness of my heart, so don't try to put me back under the law!' Read the entire chapter; it is about an offering or a 'gift' and nothing to do with tithing. Giving out of the goodness of your heart sounds very spiritual but don't get overly optimistic about the goodness of your heart. Even though we are believers in Christ, we are still natural-born sinners, and we retain the sin nature even after the new birth. Tithing tethers us to God in acknowledging him with our first fruits, not the leftovers. Tithing is the outward sign of my devotion and affection towards God and his house. Tithing is proof that I have come into covenant with God as the real Lord of my life. Tithing shows he is Master, not me, not MasterCard but Jesus! Tithing is the visible proof that I have set my priorities up correctly, God first and none other.

Some people say, 'Oh, I give everything I have to God.' This sounds good, but I wish I could look at their actual giving to see what the goodness of their hearts actually look like in real life. I think I already know the results!

This scripture is not about tithing, but about offerings. They are distinctly different from the consistent tithe of a flat 10% of your increase paid out of discipline and principle.

Tithing is the foundation for giving, though not the entire picture of giving. The offering is different in that it is a discretionary amount, purposed in your heart. The offerings are flexible and come from the heart of the giver.

Offerings are all about a 'gift' relationship with God, whereas the tithe is about a 'trust' relationship with God. Offerings – any money that is given willingly – are from the heart of the giver. It is a statement of love and gratitude. As an example of an offering given cheerfully, in 1 Chronicles 29:9 the people rejoiced at the willing response of their leaders, for they had given freely and whole-heartedly to the Lord. David the king also rejoiced greatly. If you read the full chapter you will see that millions were given in order to build the temple, God's house.

For the offering, you determine the amount and where to give it, guided by your heart, out of your own resources. This is what Paul meant when he spoke in 2 Corinthians 9:6–7.

We do not operate under the Mosaic Law but we still operate under God's law. This is not a set of rules and regulations, or about religion putting us on a guilt trip, but the heart of God, the mind of God and the nature of God. God's giving nature is summed up by his love for us in that he gave his Son to us – John 3:16.

CHAPTER 5

Born to be Blessed

When I first became a Christian I looked around my local church and something struck me. I heard people preach about how God desires to bless and prosper us, but I did not see much prosperity. I had seen much more wealth among the Jewish community.

This puzzled me – especially as a young Messianic Jew – and I began to search the Scriptures for a possible reason. I had no particular desire to be poor and wanted to understand how, as a Christian, I could live in the blessing of God. This is what I discovered.

In Genesis chapter 12, God made a covenant with Abraham. God chose to call out a special people for himself through whom he would bring blessing to all nations. The covenant, detailed in verses 1–3, heralded the beginning of this process and spoke about three main things:

1. **The promise of land.** God called Abraham from Ur of the Chaldees to a land he would give him.
2. **The promise of descendants (or seed).** God promised that out of Abraham would come a great nation. This

promise would culminate in the appearance of a Messiah in the line of David.

3. **The promise of blessing and redemption.** God promised to bless Abraham and the families of the earth through him.

Jewish people are born into this Abrahamic covenant by default. As such, they inherit the blessing that God decreed through his covenant. But as Christians, we are also brought under this covenantal blessing. The Apostle Paul explains in Romans 4 how Abraham, by virtue of his faith in God, became the father of all those who believe, whether circumcised (Jew) or uncircumcised (Gentile).

In Galatians 3:9, Paul states that, '*So then those who are of faith are blessed with believing Abraham.*' And if there is still any doubt, Paul seals the matter in Galatians 3:29: '*If you are Christ's, then you are Abraham's seed, and heirs according to the promise.*'

As believers we are heirs of God's promise. Being an heir means that there is something to inherit! Why then do some people, notably the Jewish community, seem to thrive under this blessing, whereas others have a hit-or-miss experience of God's blessing? If Christians are just as much the heirs of God's promises, what are we doing that is different? I believe it has to do with a lack of understanding of the root of God's blessing.

Do you want the root or the fruit?
In Genesis 25:5–6 (NIV):

Abraham left everything he owned to Isaac. But while he was still living, he gave gifts to the sons of his concubines and sent them away from his son Isaac to the land of the east.

We read about Abraham passing on God's blessing to his son, Isaac. It simply reads, '*And Abraham gave all that he had to Isaac.*'

Abraham knew he was about to die, so he blessed Isaac with a rich inheritance. Isaac was the promised son, the chosen one, and so was in line for this blessing. But Abraham had more children than just Isaac – so what about them? We read that Abraham also gave gifts to the sons he fathered with his concubine. If he gave Isaac ALL, then what would have been left over? There was a difference in what Abraham gave to Isaac and what he gave to the other children.

Later we read in verse 11 that after the death of Abraham, '*God blessed his son Isaac*'. God was honouring the covenant he made with Abraham and blessing the first in line of his descendants. We see the extraordinary effect of this covenant blessing in the very next chapter.

Genesis 26:1 tells us that, '*There was a famine in the land . . .*' I see this as akin to the economic meltdown that the world is currently experiencing. There was serious trouble and people were experiencing great hardship. Yet look at what was happening with Isaac:

Isaac sowed in that land, and in the same year reaped a hundred-fold; and the LORD blessed him. The man began to prosper, and continued prospering until he became very prosperous; for he had possessions of flocks . . . herds and a great number of servants. So the Philistines envied him.
(Genesis 26:12–14)

This is fascinating. Isaac is prospering in the midst of an economic crisis – and not only a little; he is thriving, not just surviving! Why is this?

Look again at the transaction that happened between Abraham and Isaac. Abraham gave all he had to Isaac and only gifts to his other children. What Abraham gave to Isaac was the 'root' and not just the 'fruit'.

The *root* of God's blessing is the God-given ability to work, to produce, to be creative, and to create wealth. The fruit is what is produced out of that. A key reason why the Jewish people prosper as they do is because they focus on the root and not the fruit. Others fall for the trap of focusing only on the fruit – but we can't create fruit without the root.

The fruit is just the outer, visual expression of the root; it comes out of the blessing itself. When Jesus taught, what scriptures did he use? Genesis, Exodus, etc., and certainly not Philippians and the gospels – they were not written yet. Jesus understood this principle of root rather than fruit.

In Matthew 6:24–33 Jesus again is dealing with money. He continues to address the area of fruit in our lives – eating and drinking and clothing – but effectively says, *'Don't worry about what you will eat, drink and wear – this is what the Gentiles seek! – but seek first the kingdom of God (the root) and all those things (fruit) shall be added to you!'*

In Deuteronomy 8, God specifically warns against forgetting where the source of our prosperity comes from. Instead we need to remember to keep God central to our lives.

> *Beware that you do not forget the LORD your God . . . then you say in your heart, 'My power and the might of my hand have gained me this wealth.'*
> (Deuteronomy 8:11, 17)

When the Lord appeared to Solomon in a dream-vision and said to him, *'Ask for whatever you want me to give you'*

(1 Kings 3:5 NIV), Solomon could have rattled off a shopping list of requests that basically represented fruit: riches, good health, a long life etc. But instead he focused on the root. He asked for godly wisdom:

Give to your servant an understanding heart to judge your people, that I may discern between good and evil.
(verse 9)

Solomon knew that if he could tap into the root and connect with the mind of God, then blessing would flow naturally out of that place of alignment. It is amazing what happens when you align your thoughts, actions and feelings with God's ways.

Look at God's response to this:

Because you have asked this thing, and have not asked long life for yourself, nor have asked riches for yourself, nor have asked the life of your enemies, but have asked for yourself understanding to discern justice, behold, I have done according to your words; see, I have given you a wise and understanding heart, so that there has not been anyone like you before you, nor shall any like you arise after you.

And I have also given you what you have not asked: both riches and honour, so that there shall not be anyone like you among the kings all your days. So if you walk in my ways, to keep my statutes and my commandments, as your father David walked, then I will lengthen your days.
(1 Kings 3:11–14)

God was pleased with Solomon's request for the root and he granted it, but then he blessed him with the fruit anyway.

So often in life people pursue the fruit and neglect the root. They run after fruit because it appears quick and easy to acquire, offering a comfortable lifestyle with very little commitment. Attending to the root – pursuing God, his presence, and putting him at the centre of our life – takes more effort and time. It's not a quick fix, but a lifestyle.

The root speaks of covenant, foundation and stability. Growing and maintaining the root is a long term commitment. Fruit is only a short-term solution.

The same principle applies in business. Most people who go into business expect to reap fruit from their venture almost immediately – like a job: you go to work and at the end of the week or month you get paid. But the root and fruit principle comes into play here. Look at these verses in Leviticus:

> *When you enter the land and plant any kind of fruit tree, regard its fruit as forbidden. For three years you are to consider it forbidden; it must not be eaten. In the fourth year all its fruit will be holy, an offering of praise to the LORD. But in the fifth year you may eat its fruit. In this way your harvest will be increased. I am the LORD your God.*
> (Leviticus 19:23–25 NIV)

In other words, God is counselling us to focus on the root, not the fruit. To grow a successful business you need to nurture it and count on the first three years being pretty slim. Don't be tempted to immediately eat all the fruit it produces. You will see the benefit of what you have sown in the fourth and fifth years if you grow it the right way.

This ubiquitous 'want it now' mind-set is contrary to Scripture. If we want to enjoy the blessing and prosperity promised by God to all the seed of Abraham, then we need to be root people and not fruit people. We need to be those who are focused on God, the giver of gifts, not the gifts themselves. We need to worship the God whose heart is to prosper us, not worship prosperity itself.

The real purpose of wealth

When we align ourselves with God's way of thinking we begin to view wealth in a completely different light. If our focus is on the root and not the fruit – on God, the one who blesses us with the ability to create wealth, and not on the wealth itself – then our financial resources take on new purpose.

The real purpose of wealth is fourfold:

1. To provide for our family.
2. To bless others.
3. To extend God's kingdom on the earth.
4. So that we might become influencers for God in the lives of others.

Blessed to be a blessing

When we see that, first of all, we are just stewards of the resources we have, which actually belong to God, and secondly that it is God's heart to be generous towards others, we will understand that we are *blessed to be a blessing*.

Money takes on a new meaning once we look beyond our own needs being met. This is why it is so important to have a financially stable life. As you build your own financial house you will find a peace about money, and you will not just tithe but overflow to give as God touches your heart.

The real purpose of wealth is not simply to enable us to do things for ourselves; it is also to do things for others.

Prosperity must never be purely self-consuming. It must help others and be outwardly, not inwardly focused.

Be careful that you do not forget the LORD your God, failing to observe his commands, his laws and his decrees that I am giving you this day. Otherwise, when you eat and are satisfied, when you build fine houses and settle down, and when your herds and flocks grow large and your silver and gold increase and all you have is multiplied, then your heart will become proud and you will forget the LORD your God, who brought you out of Egypt, out of the land of slavery.
(Deuteronomy 8:11–14 NIV)

Giving is a part of getting; in fact, giving is the first step. Do you want to have more? Then give more!
Jesus spelled out for us the key equations of biblical economics:

Give, and it will be given to you: good measure, pressed down, shaken together, and running over will be put into your bosom. For with the same measure that you use, it will be measured back to you.
(Luke 6:38)

For whoever has, to him more will be given, and he will have abundance; but whoever does not have, even what he has will be taken away from him.
(Matthew 13:12)

The world cannot understand how, if you give more away, you get more back; it makes no sense. But biblical economics do not work like worldly economics. Nevertheless , we still need to do things with financial intelligence.

God has blessed me in business and I enjoy a nice lifestyle, but I do not live an extravagant lifestyle. I drive a car that is thirteen years old. I do not spend a lot of money on unnecessary material things.

God has helped me to understand that what I have is his; he just allows me to look after it. If I were to selfishly consume it all on myself, then it would be gone and that would be that. But if I allow myself to be a conduit of God's blessing to others, then God keeps on pouring more and more in, so that there is an overflow.

However you give and whatever causes you choose to support, make sure that you do not just consume all your resources yourself. Instead, live in the overflow of God's blessing. You do not need to feel guilty about having a nice lifestyle, just do not get caught up in it. Never live for money alone or you may find yourself like the miser Scrooge, all alone. A real key is to not let your self-worth be valued by your net worth. Your worth to God is priceless!

Resourcing God's kingdom

As well as being a blessing to those around us, we should begin to see the bigger picture of God's agenda for his world. Issues of justice and mercy begin to affect our giving as we see the need that exists in the world and understand God's heart for the poor.

I love being a part of my local church in London, where the culture is that we live beyond ourselves (not beyond our means). I know that when I give it will support the local ministries, but also needs further afield. The money is going to help give somebody clean water in Uganda, or contribute to one of the many mission causes that are a part of our focus.

It makes me want to generate more wealth because there is so much need that has to be addressed. I want to be wealthier, not necessarily so that I can drive a better car or live in a bigger house, but so I can become a bigger person – a kingdom person.

Chapter 29 of 1 Chronicles provides a list of all the wealth that was gathered in to facilitate the building of the temple of the Lord. It is a beautiful picture of the people of God directing their wealth into building God's house. In the same way, we are to pool our respective resources so that the church we are part of can extend God's kingdom and touch the lives of those in our community and beyond.

Verse 9 of this passage always touches me:

Then the people rejoiced, for they had offered willingly, because with a loyal heart they had offered willingly to the LORD.

What a joy it is when people give freely. In verse 12 we read of God's response to our willingness:

Both riches and honour come from you,
and you reign over all . . .
in your hand it is to make great
and to give strength to all.

God wants to give us wealth. It varies in proportion – not everyone will become a millionaire. But when we are rich in good works, God rewards us richly. Money is the extension of the real you! It takes on your nature.

Becoming an influencer

Some years ago my wife, Margo, and I made plans to retire early and move to the south of France. I was going to sell my part of the business and just keep up the occasional speaking engagement. God, however, had other plans.

Back when I had no money, I told God that if I could learn about the 'mysteries' of money I would invest my life into educating others about true, biblical prosperity. It is easy to make promises to God when you are broke – you have nothing to lose. But, of course, when God has upheld his end of the bargain, then you need to uphold yours.

Upholding this pledge means operating by principle, and not by my emotions. My emotions say, *'Hey, you don't need to travel and share this message about financial independence. Go to the beach. You have been working hard and you deserve a few years off.'*

But it is interesting that there is no word in Hebrew for retirement. God wants us all to be givers and continue to contribute.

My character and appreciation for all God has done for me whispers in my ear, *'Remember the promise you made. There are hurting people out there who need to hear the message of how God's economy works. Don't just be a taker – be a giver.'*

So, I pack my bags and go where I feel the right doors (not every open door is the right door) are opened. That is why I have written this book. I know the blessings of God, and want to help as many of God's people as I can to reach their full potential. Nothing brings me greater joy than seeing people grow in all four areas of their lives and living a larger life than they thought possible. We need kingdom-minded people to rise up in their individual gifting and help to finance and further kingdom-minded projects.

I had also wondered about becoming more involved in the leadership of a church. But I chatted to a pastor friend about this and he reminded me of how many people I had managed to lead to the Lord in the course of my business. 'Jeff,' he said, 'I think God wants you just where you are – where you can continue to touch people's lives.' He was right.

It would be so easy to just sit on the beach and soak up the sunshine, but actually, with wealth comes the ability to influence others for good. If there were two speakers on soapboxes on opposing corners of a street – one speaking about how to get saved and the other speaking about how to become a millionaire – which one would have the bigger crowd around them? With wealth comes a greater responsibility to remain a good steward over our time and resources.

The way the world works is that people notice those who have become prosperous and afford them credibility. People listen to you; you can command their attention. With that influence there is the opportunity to share the gospel: to share simply about your faith and how it has affected the course of your life. I have seen many people respond to God as I have shared my testimony with them – and that in the midst of discussing their finances.

This is prosperity with purpose: to be a blessing to others, to extend the kingdom and influence others to seek Christ for themselves. The purpose of prosperity is that we are blessed to be a blessing.

CHAPTER 6

Changing your Money Mind-Set

I hope that I have helped you to change or at least challenged the way you think about money. I also hope that thinking differently has provoked you to action regarding your stewardship of the resources God has placed in your hands. On the road to financial freedom we must learn to be givers, not getters; to remember that we are blessed to be a blessing to others. God's blessing is not simply for us to consume ourselves.

Dr Benjamin A. Rogge, a free-market economist and founder of the Foundation for Economic Education, said:

> Rich men know how to make money, but they are seldom very skilled in giving it away.

Rogge defined his role in the multi-million dollar foundation quite simply: 'To see to it that the money is spent in ways that will not produce more harm than good.' He saw something of the truth about prosperity and of being a good steward, and identified that we are truly rich when we use our God-given resources to help meet the needs of others.

This scripture sums up the biblical mind-set and adds the following warning:

When you have eaten and are full, then you shall bless the LORD *your God for the good land which he has given you. Beware that you do not forget the* LORD *your God by not keeping his commandments, his judgments, and his statutes which I command you today, lest – when you have eaten and are full, and have built beautiful houses and dwell in them; and when your herds and your flocks multiply, and your silver and your gold are multiplied, and all that you have is multiplied; when your heart is lifted up, and you forget the* LORD *your God . . .*
(Deuteronomy 8:10–14)

Here we clearly see that:

- God commands a blessing on our lives and resources.
- While we are enjoying the blessing we must not forget God, our source; we need to stay thankful.
- God wants us to live in overflow, so that we are a blessing to others.
- We are warned against just consuming only for our own benefit.

In case there is any doubt: yes, it is God's will to multiply everything you have that you place under his care. Yes, it is God's will for you to have more than enough, so that you can share it with others.

But there are other, very important areas to address about money – and one of them is debt. In the chapters that follow I offer some tried and tested practical advice for godly financial management. But the first step in any plan that moves towards financial freedom must be to think differently about debt.

To me, debt is simply robbing our future finances (plus interest) to pay for the present because we don't have the self-discipline or patience to live within our means. When we buy things we really cannot afford we are just 'playing house,' and not doing ourselves any favours in the long term.

Creating an anti-debt culture

Proverbs 22:6 is one of the most quoted Bible verses when it comes to the topic of parenting:

Train up a child in the way he should go,
And when he is old he will not depart from it.

This is a great general principle, but the context is not actually about parenting – it is about finances. Look at this statement in the context of its surrounding verses:

A good name is to be chosen rather than great riches,
Loving favour rather than silver and gold.
The rich and the poor have this in common,
The LORD is the maker of them all.
A prudent man foresees evil and hides himself,
But the simple pass on and are punished.
By humility and the fear of the LORD
Are riches and honour and life.
Thorns and snares are in the way of the perverse;
He who guards his soul will be far from them.
Train up a child in the way he should go,
And when he is old he will not depart from it.
The rich rules over the poor,
And the borrower is servant to the lender.

He who sows iniquity will reap sorrow,
And the rod of his anger will fail.
He who has a generous eye will be blessed,
For he gives of his bread to the poor.
(Proverbs 22:1–9)

This passage is full of godly wisdom and insight. In it we see the holistic pattern we have been discussing throughout this book, with our spiritual life, relationships, health and finances all in harmony. When these are all submitted to God there is humility and the fear of the Lord. This is what produces riches, honour and life.

To the Jewish reader, verse 6 is not just general parenting advice, but is about educating their kids how to handle money, beginning in the home. Why is it that although the Jewish people account for less than 2% of global population, they manage a disproportionate amount of the world's wealth? I believe it's because they grasp these principles of biblical economics and God continues to bless them.

Jewish families operate with an anti-debt mind set based on biblical truth. They are raised in an anti-debt culture. Let me explain the fundamental difference between a Jewish household and that of the average family in the West.

In non-Jewish families the kids wake up each morning in their mortgaged beds, put on their mortgaged clothes and go downstairs to eat breakfast at their mortgaged table. Then their parents hustle them into their mortgaged car and drive them to school. Later they return home and eat at the mortgaged table again before spending time watching their mortgaged television before bedtime. Significantly, time at the table is not spent talking about money, but other issues.

Though there are exceptions to the rule, by and large the

West lives with a have-it-now, pay-later, debt-orientated mind-set. Much of the material stuff of life is bought on credit cards or through store finance deals. High levels of debt are an accepted way of life. The banks and credit card companies have done a great job sucking us into a devilish plan of so-called 'easy' monthly payments.

The main question has become 'How can I manage my debt effectively?' rather than, 'How can I learn to live debt-free?' Getting rid of debt is one thing, but changing your mind about debt and taking a new approach is something entirely different.

Our attitudes to debt are very much learned from our parents, our chief role models as we grow up. Debt becomes a generational problem because no one showed us a better way. Some parents give out advice to their kids that they do not heed themselves, but kids are not stupid – they see when a parent's actions do not match their words. This is how we 'train up' our children. If we are comfortable with debt, so will they be.

You may be asking at this point, 'What's so bad about debt anyway – as long as it's managed?' The answer is in the scripture we have just read:

> *The rich rules over the poor,*
> *And the borrower is servant to the lender.*
> (Proverbs 22:7)

Here are some of the implications of debt:

- Debt means that someone else is controlling your finances, not you.
- Debt means that you are not being a good steward of your resources, because you are living beyond your

means. How about flowing against the culture of the day and living below your means for a change?

- Debt allows you to pretend you are someone you are not.
- The Bible cautions against charging and paying exorbitant interest rates on loans (see the advice of Exodus 22 and Deuteronomy 23).
- Debt limits your future potential to create wealth.
- Debt does not just hurt you financially, it can hurt you in ways you may not immediately appreciate. Being in debt is a known cause of stress, anxiety and depression.
- Debt can affect your health and relationships. Many marital problems and divorces can be traced back to debt and financial pressures.
- Debt affects how generous we can be in giving and funding great causes.
- Significant debt will affect things such as where you can afford to live, which in turn will impact family life and issues such as education and quality of life.

Good role models
In most Jewish families the talk around the table at mealtimes will often tend towards discussing money matters. I do not necessarily mean what happened on the stock exchange that day or the rise and fall of the real estate market; rather, biblical wisdom is shared in a natural, organic way. Practical, real-life situations and a debt-free approach to those situations are discussed.

Perhaps one of the most powerful tools a Jewish family has is its willingness to talk about money issues openly – in contrast to many Western families where money has historically been regarded as a personal matter, distasteful to discuss publicly or, worse still, 'something the children don't need to know/worry about'. How is a child supposed to learn about what is hidden from them? If you do not teach them, the advertising world will.

The talk in a Jewish household, for instance, might be about cars. 'Never buy a new car. As soon as you drive it away it will lose 20% of its value. Why would you do that? Let someone else lose that money. You buy that same car when it is a year old and save your money!'

The only reason a Jewish family will go into debt is for a property mortgage or for a loan to provide leverage for a business to make money. They certainly would not go out and buy a new car on a payment plan.

What would happen if we could get the body of Christ debt-free? The interest we pay on loans could no doubt fund a great expansion of the kingdom. Imagine a debt-free church full of debt-free families.

I remember once helping a young man to work out a financial game plan for his life that would move him towards financial freedom. I suggested that God could run his finances much better than he could, if he would entrust them to him and also honour God by tithing regularly.

The young man's response was, 'I can't afford to tithe!' As we looked at his finances together, I noticed that his monthly car finance payment was £800. We were sitting in his front room and there on his drive was a £40,000 vehicle.

I told him, 'Actually, you can afford to tithe. The problem is sitting on your driveway. That is where your tithe is, right there.'

To his credit, that guy sold his brand-new, £40,000 car and bought a similar one that was a little older, with a few more miles on the clock, for just £11,000 – and paid cash for it. Then he began tithing. It was amazing what happened to him after that. Within a couple of weeks his boss gave him a large pay increase out of the blue.

I still see him occasionally and every time I do he gives me a big hug. I was not trying to criticise him or hurt him by telling him to get rid of his fancy car, I was trying to help him to come into alignment with the blessing of God – to see God open the windows of heaven over his life. God honoured his obedience.

In life we need great role models. Many people envy or despise successful people, but why not learn from them and copy them? I was blessed to have a great mentor in business.

I met Bob when I was twenty-four. He came from a poor background, but had worked his way up in the world of financial services to the point where he was a multi-millionaire. He has a deep love for the Lord and a heart for the things of God. When I asked him how he became wealthy, Bob asked me very simply, 'Would you like to be wealthy?' I told him yes and he said, 'Well, copy me then.'

So that is what I did. I copied Bob and eventually became a millionaire in my own right. I wish I could tell you that I am some kind of creative genius, but I did not come up with the ideas, I just copied someone else. Being willing to learn and aligning yourself with a good role model is so important. It requires having a teachable heart.

I have heard it said that Jewish people are good with money because it is 'in their DNA.' There may be an element of truth to this. It is true, as we saw in the previous chapter, that the Jewish nation has inherited the blessing of God for continued prosperity. In that sense it is very much part of their DNA as a people group. But in addition, they apply godly principles to their life and business; they are hard-working, industrious people.

It is an interesting fact that many millionaires own their own businesses and tend to be extremely hardworking people. Not all business owners become millionaires, of course, but you stand a better chance of creating more wealth for you and your family if you work for yourself rather than someone else.

My grandfather moved to the US from Lithuania looking for work and eventually decided to start running his own grocery business. He and my grandmother had an apartment above the shop. At 6 o'clock every evening my grandfather would go upstairs, get his dinner and catch two hours of sleep while my grandmother watched the store. Then from 8 pm onwards he would place a chair close to the door and sleep in the chair. If he heard the shop door hit the chair he would get up and serve the customer – so it was effectively a 24-hour store.

The morality of money making

For some people, the making of money and high moral values are mutually exclusive. Making money is associated with sharp practices and perhaps a lack of integrity – raw commercialism at its worst. Wealth creation has a bad press – and an increasing number of revelations in the media regarding the banking industry do nothing to change people's perception that it is all about greed at someone else's expense.

But wealth creation, if it happens under God's guidance, is not immoral at all. In the Jewish faith, doing business is seen as inherently good and spiritual. It is viewed as a noble activity because the only way to make money is to serve the needs of other human beings. It is morally sound because it is putting to good use the ability God has given us to create wealth and prosper.

We are being good stewards of our talents and abilities when we put them to work and seek to use them to glorify God. We are created in his image. This means we should go forth and multiply, and be faithful in every area of our lives. One of the biggest mistakes Christian businesspeople make is to separate the spiritual from the secular – dealing with business as though it is somehow unspiritual.

I believe this is one reason why so many churches find it hard to reach out to business people in the community. Some church leaders tend to view them only in terms of what cash they contribute to the running of the church. While I believe in helping to resource God's kingdom, we should also celebrate those among us who work hard and contribute to the local economy.

Entrepreneurs can contribute not just financially but by emotional intelligence. They are smart and enterprising people. We need to reach out to them, just like anyone else, love them for who they are, and respect the gifts that they have.

I was once in a church meeting where the preacher spoke out against making money for the creation of wealth . . . and then took an offering! That doesn't make any sense to me. Instead we should be seeking to empower the entrepreneurs in our churches and give them the tools they need to be effective witnesses in the marketplace.

Creating wealth is a godly exercise when it is done to meet the needs of others. The quest for wealth for wealth's sake alone leads nowhere. But when it is done in alignment with God's Word, according to biblical principles, it results in an amazing kingdom overflow that touches the lives of countless people.

It was Winston Churchill who said:

Occasionally, a man stumbles over the truth. Most dust themselves off and continue walking as though nothing had happened.

Let us not be like that and miss these valuable principles that God has given us to succeed in life.

It was also Churchill who so aptly put it:

What is the use of living, if it be not to strive for noble causes and to make this muddled world a better place for those who will live in it after we are gone?

Let us learn to live within our means, but also to live beyond ourselves. One of the first steps is to become debt-free.

CHAPTER 7

The Financial Position of Jesus

Consider for a moment that Jesus is a Jew, and if he was on earth today, he would still be a Jew. People often ask me if I am Jewish or a Christian. I respond by asking 'What was Jesus? He was Jewish, right?'

So, what does the word Christian mean? It means 'like Christ,' so if you are a Christian, I guess that makes you Jewish. God's Word says if you believe in *Y'shua* (Jesus' Hebrew name), then you have been grafted into the vine and are now of the seed of Abraham.

Jesus was the pattern Son of God, and God owns all the resources of the world. Yet we are convinced that Jesus was poor, even though he was Jewish. Why do we have to think of him as a pauper? What scriptural basis is there to show that Jesus and his disciples were poor?

I have two stories to paint for you and ask which one takes more faith to believe.

Story number one goes like this:

2,000 years ago there was a Jewish boy who lived in Israel who was given much wealth when he was only a very small child. His parents watched over this money and even used some of it as living expenses while living in Egypt. He followed his stepfather's trade as a carpenter and was a successful, well-respected businessman in the community. He was financially astute and had a great reputation, growing in favour with God and man.

As the eldest son, he inherited his stepfather's home, assets and business. When he went into ministry at age 30, money was not an issue because he had planned ahead, saved money and was a good steward. He had plenty of financially stable friends who supported his ministry.

He had his life together when it came to relationships, health, finances and his spiritual life. He practised what he preached and although money was not the central theme to his life, it was managed well in order to set an example for those who followed him.

Why could this have not been true?

Here is story number two, a real whopper of a tale:

Two thousand years ago there was a Jewish boy born of a virgin. He lived in Israel and at age thirty he started a ministry, and for three and a half years gathered followers from the Jewish community.

He performed miracles like raising people from the dead, opening blind eyes, healing the lame and casting out demons. Once he even turned the water into wine when he was attending a wedding reception and on another occasion, he walked on water, commanding the stormy weather to be still.

This man was beaten, crucified and died but three days later he rose from the dead and then ascended into the sky. The good news is that he plans to return to the earth some day and rule the earth forever and ever. Oh yes, and he also happens to be the Son of God. If you believe in him, you too can have eternal life.

Which one of these two stories is harder to believe? Why can't both of them be true?

So, what was Jesus' financial situation? Many people quote Luke 9:58 to say that Jesus had no home but wandered about:

Jesus replied: 'Foxes have dens and birds have nests, but the Son of Man has nowhere to lay his head.'
(Luke 9:58 NIV)

Let's read the context in Luke 9:51–58 (NIV):

As the time approached for him to be taken up to heaven, Jesus resolutely set out for Jerusalem. And he sent messengers on ahead, who went into a Samaritan village to get things ready for him; but the people there did not welcome him, because he was heading for Jerusalem.

When the disciples James and John saw this, they asked, 'Lord, do you want us to call fire down from heaven to destroy them?' But Jesus turned and rebuked them. Then he and his disciples went to another village.

As they were walking along the road, a man said to him, 'I will follow you wherever you go.' Jesus replied, 'Foxes have dens and birds have nests, but the Son of Man has no place to lay his head.'

The messengers went before Jesus as envoys to set things up, but were not received: they couldn't get a reservation or meeting room. So they moved out and went to another village. As they were leaving, a man asked to go with him and Jesus replied that there was no bed for that night. He was pointing out that the ministry takes dedication and focus and is not for the fainthearted.

Jesus was on the road at times and not everyone received him but he had a house he could return to. In Mark 2:1–2 he was in his house. Later in the chapter the roof is taken off of the house to let the crippled man down, in his bed. Then in Mark 2:14–15 Jesus left his house and went to Levi's house to sit and eat.

In Mark 9:33, he was in the house at Capernaum. In Luke 7:1, after a full schedule of preaching he went home to Capernaum. In Matthew 17:23–27, Peter went to catch a fish to get a gold coin to pay taxes. Look at verse 24 – they came to Capernaum (a town on the north coast of Lake Galilee). Verse 25 talks about him coming into the house.

I could go on but hopefully you have got the point that the Messiah had stability in his life and was not a vagrant, begging or depending on charity.

Now look at John 12:1–8 (NIV):

Six days before the Passover, Jesus came to Bethany, where Lazarus lived, whom Jesus had raised from the dead. Here a dinner was given in Jesus' honour. Martha served, while Lazarus was among those reclining at the table with him. Then Mary took about a pint of pure nard, an expensive perfume; she poured it on Jesus' feet and wiped his feet with her hair. And the house was filled with the fragrance of the perfume.

But one of his disciples, Judas Iscariot, who was later to betray him, objected, 'Why wasn't this perfume sold and the money given to the poor? It was worth a year's wages.' He did not say this because he cared about the poor but because he was a thief; as keeper of the money bag, he used to help himself to what was put into it.

'Leave her alone,' Jesus replied. 'It was intended that she should save this perfume for the day of my burial. You will always have the poor among you, but you will not always have me.'

If Jesus' attitude about money was about scarcity or a poverty mentality, why did he not reprimand Mary for using this costly oil? He was aware of the poor people and even remarked that they are with us always. If Jesus and his disciples were a threadbare bunch of beggars, no doubt they would have taken this costly ointment and sold it just to exist for another day.

Jesus' net worth

Jesus was not poor in any area of his life. He had his act together. The religious world has painted a picture of Jesus as a humble, penniless man, dismissive of material possessions, who surrounded himself with equally poor disciples. It conjures images of a destitute band wandering around the countryside begging for bread, dependent on charity and hand-outs. Jesus may have possessed incredible humility, but poor he was not.

I have a sneaking suspicion that the religious would like Jesus to be poor so that they can use him as evidence in a case study to discredit those who possess wealth and yet claim to be spiritually sound – something that tends to jar with the religious mind-set. I aim to demonstrate that this is simply not true.

You cannot exert influence in this world without money, because money makes this world go around, as the saying goes.

A feast is made for laughter,
  wine makes life merry,
  and money is the answer for everything.
(Ecclesiastes 10:19 NIV)

Other than the one thing in life it cannot account for – the issue of our eternal salvation – money can pretty much solve every other problem. With wealth comes influence. Earlier, the writer of Ecclesiastes has this to say:

There was once a small city with only a few people in it. And a powerful king came against it, surrounded it and built huge siege works against it.Now there lived in that city a man poor but wise, and he saved the city by his wisdom. But nobody remembered that poor man.
(Ecclesiastes 9:14–15 NIV)

Although this poor wise man saved a city, no one remembered him. He was poor, unremarkable, undistinguished. Whatever he did for this city, he failed to leave an impression. He had no influence. Conversely, we read in Deuteronomy 8:18 NIV):

But remember the LORD your God, for it is he who gives you the ability to produce wealth, and so confirms his covenant, which he swore to your ancestors, as it is today.

The New Living Translation renders this as, *'the power to be successful'.* It can also be seen as 'the power to get results' and carries the same meaning as 'influential'. In essence, if we want to be able to exert a positive influence on our communities it is going to require wealth. Outreaches and missions need funding to work properly. Ministries do not run on thin air and goodwill. The operation of God's kingdom requires finance.

Jesus had a trust fund

Just as any good natural father would not send his son on an around-the-world trip without first making sure he had enough money to provide for his needs, so God the Father cared for his Son. He would not send Jesus into the world and later ask him to conduct an extensive missions programme without making provision for it.

We can tell from reading the gospels that Jesus understood his Father's commitment to underwrite all his activities, from his implicit trust in that provision. Whenever he needed something, he went to his Father and asked for it.

It is amazing how misleading and unbiblical the world's view of Jesus can be. Soft-focus Christmas images of a baby in a manger and poor Mary and Joseph flanked by a donkey, a cow, and three kings spring to mind. Reading the gospel accounts, we discover something different, and several revealing facts come to light.

In Luke 2:1–5 they went to Bethlehem to pay taxes. It takes money and earnings to pay taxes. Then, we see in Luke 2:7 that the family did not end up in a stable because they were poor and wretched. It was just because everywhere else was fully booked. Joseph had the money to pay for accommodation. He was not broke.

Do you think God would appoint as Jesus' step-father, a key influence in his formative years, someone who was destitute? I do not think so. Also, Joseph was a carpenter. He was a craftsman; he had a respected trade to his name. He ran his own successful business and he later passed on the skills and knowledge of his trade to his son. A carpenter back then meant a 'master builder'.

Secondly, we see that Mary rode a donkey on that journey into Bethlehem. Read in the light of our modern context that might sound poor, because it conjures up a picture of basic, rural simplicity. But back in the day, riding a donkey was like driving a car. Generally speaking, a poor, pregnant woman would walk everywhere.

Thirdly, we discover that the 'wise men from the East' were never at the manger. In fact, they visited Jesus at Mary and Joseph's house. Then we see God's provision arriving for Jesus' early years. Although the Bible freely skips from the events of the inn to this scene at the family home, in fact Jesus was approximately two years old at this point.

> *And when they had come into the **house**, they saw the young child with Mary his mother, and fell down and worshipped him. And when they had opened their treasures, they presented gifts to him: gold, frankincense, and myrrh.*
> (Matthew 2:11, emphasis added)

The 'wise men' (it does not ever say that there were three) are revealed as kings. They didn't just present Jesus with some nice gifts; they brought treasure in recognition of this unique child.

They acknowledged the fact that Jesus was a king and as such brought gifts fit for a king. If you were taking a gift to a king you would not take an old toaster! If you were a king you would bring something of great value. In today's money, the gifts they brought could have been worth millions of pounds.

Suddenly Joseph had been given amazing, abundant provision to care for his family. Being a good Jewish man, Joseph would have understood the need to create an inheritance fund for his children. He did not squander this wealth on lavish living.

A good man leaves an inheritance to his children's children,
But the wealth of the sinner is stored up for the righteous.
(Proverbs 13:22)

Soon after the wise men came (Matthew 2:13) an angel appeared to Joseph and tells him to flee and live in Egypt. How did he survive there financially? He had Jesus' 'trust fund' to live on and saved the rest as an inheritance. As such, Jesus was well cared for and wanted for nothing. His parents would have practised the saying, *'train up your child the way he should go'* (Proverbs 22:6), including in the area of finances!

Provision for the disciples
Being a good steward meant Peter would have rented out his fishing boats to others or put in place a manager to run his fishing operation while he was travelling and ministering with Jesus. This would have been a logical thing to do for a man who was a good steward of his resources. He would not have abandoned his business and walked off with Jesus as some seem to think.

In Luke 9:3 we read Jesus' advice to his disciples who are hitting the road to minister throughout the surrounding villages:

And he said to them, 'Take nothing for the journey, neither staffs nor bag nor bread nor money; and do not have two tunics apiece.'

You do not have to tell poor people with no money not to bring any money! I do not believe Jesus said this because they had no money between them – far from it. Jesus had a deeper reason: he was teaching them how to rely on God and operate in faith.

He wanted to teach them that they needed to lean on God for *everything* they needed to live and operate – not just for the spiritual power that was needed to minister. They had money, but he wanted them to see beyond it and realise that all provision comes from the Father. So they would travel and take little with them, reliant upon God to provide.

Later we see Jesus say something totally different to them:

And he said to them, 'When I sent you without money bag, knapsack, and sandals, did you lack anything?' So they said, 'Nothing.' Then he said to them, 'But now, he who has a money bag, let him take it, and likewise a knapsack . . .'
(Luke 22:35–36)

First Jesus tells them to take nothing because he is teaching them dependence on the Father. Now he is telling them to take money and other provisions with them on the road.

At this point Jesus was giving his disciples a new commission: the time was imminent for them to go out into the world. Soon they would be travelling around ministering without Jesus in an often hostile environment. They would not be staying in friends' houses this time, so they needed finance for travel, accommodation and subsistence.

This ministry had resources to draw on. Jesus quickly had twelve full-time staff on his books, and before long seventy-two more joined the organisation. This would have required considerable funding just like a large ministry today would need 'provision for the vision.'

Jesus' donor base

After this, Jesus travelled about from one town and village to another, proclaiming the good news of the kingdom of God. The Twelve were with him, and also some women who had been cured of evil spirits and diseases: Mary (called Magdalene) from whom seven demons had come out; Joanna the wife of Chuza, the manager of Herod's household; Susanna; and many others. These women were helping to support them out of their own means.
(Luke 8:1–3 NIV)

A ministry that had a large number of people travelling through 'every' city and village conducting missions would have needed a considerable amount of money to back up its operations. In addition to their own financial resources, Jesus had financial supporters who helped to fund the work.

Joanna's husband was Herod's financial manager and would have been a wealthy lady (how ironic that Herod was indirectly funding Jesus' ministry!). Others gave to him 'out of their own means.' All the financial needs of the ministry were taken care of.

A treasurer was the only official position that Jesus had. Did he need a treasurer or accountant to handle £100? With a staff of eighty-two, eating, drinking, lodging and setting up places to have meetings were quite a logistical operation. Although we only tend to think of Judas in the context of his betrayal of Jesus, the fact is, they were handling enough money to require a treasurer. They needed an accounts person to keep track of the large amounts of money going into and out of the ministry.

As an aside, Jesus was not stupid. He knew all along that Judas was embezzling money from the ministry account, but he chose not to do anything about it. Why? I believe he was teaching his disciples a deeper lesson, that even though someone may be stealing from you, God can still provide. He can still get all the money you need to you. Although Judas was a bad steward, the ministry did not even miss the money he stole. That is how abundant their finances were.

Jesus was the eldest son

Although we are not told when it happened, the Scriptures imply that at some point, Joseph, Jesus' step-father died, leaving Jesus as head of the family as the eldest son. Under Jewish law the eldest son stood to inherit the majority of his father's estate, generally a double portion compared to his siblings. At some point, Jesus became responsible for his family and he would have taken good care of them out of his step-dad's inheritance.

Jesus also used his resources to provide for the needs of others – and abundantly so. Read afresh the account in Luke 9 of the feeding of the five thousand.

Late in the afternoon the Twelve came to him and said, 'Send the crowd away so they can go to the surrounding villages and countryside and find food and lodging, because we are in a remote place here.' He replied, 'You give them something to eat.'

*They answered, 'We have only five loaves of bread and two fish – unless we **go and buy food for all this crowd**.'(About five thousand men were there.)*

But he said to his disciples, 'Make them sit down in groups of about fifty each.' The disciples did so, and everyone sat down.

Taking the five loaves and the two fish and looking up to heaven, he gave thanks and broke them. Then he gave them

to the disciples to distribute to the people. They all ate and were satisfied, and the disciples picked up twelve basketfuls of broken pieces that were left over.
(Luke 9:12–17 NIV, emphasis added)

We always tend to focus on the miracle of food multiplication in this story – and rightly so, because it is an outstanding miracle. But it is easy to miss the fact that buying dinner for five thousand people was a viable option here. I don't believe the disciples' comment, 'unless we go and buy food for all these people' was sarcasm. If they had wanted, they possessed the funds to feed the whole assembled crowd.

Jesus' decision to call on God's miraculous power was not a financial decision, but a spiritual one. He wanted to demonstrate the Father's amazing provision again. But equally he could have taken them all to a restaurant!

Notice that there was more left over at the end than there was to begin with. This is a beautiful picture of the tithe. It is what happens when we trust our little to God. Supernaturally he expands it so that everyone is satisfied and there is more to give away on top. Jesus learnt to live in the abundant overflow of God's provision and so must we.

Lastly, if Jesus was poor, why did he wear designer clothes? John 19:23–24 tells us that the soldiers cast lots for his clothes. You do not cast lots for a shoddy garment. This garment had value and was not a cheap item. It was not a 'one size fits all'.

Jesus needed finance to survive and had no money problems. He lived under the blessing of Abraham and was a good steward over the resources given to him. He viewed money as simply a resource needed to fund the expansion of the kingdom of God.

Jesus had the *shalom* of God in all four areas of his life: spiritual, relationships, health and finance.

No, Jesus was not poor financially. He is the first-born Son and shows God's favour on his life. He is the example and pattern for us.

CHAPTER 8

Frugal Living, Extravagant Giving

'Too many people spend money they have not earned to buy things they do not want to impress people they don't like.'   (Will Smith)

In Proverbs 27:20 we find the following telling observation: *'The eyes of a man are never satisfied.'*

In this age, with its culture of commercialism and consumer choice, we ought to ask ourselves the question: *How much is enough? How much is too much to have?*

I am not telling you how to spend your money or on what. You have to decide that yourself.

Keep falsehood and lies far from me;
give me neither poverty nor riches,
but give me only my daily bread.
Otherwise, I may have too much and disown you
and say , 'Who is the LORD?'
Or I may become poor and steal,
and so dishonour the name of my God.
(Proverbs 30:8–9 NIV)

'Neither poverty or riches' – both of these are relative to the situation. You may feel impoverished because you can't have everything you want, but ask someone in Somalia who has not eaten in a few days what is poverty!

Riches are relative along with increased wealth comes increased stewardship responsibilities. So let us say, for example, you earn £40,000 per year and you would really like to become a kingdom person. You tithe and have a plan to become debt-free.

What would you need to have a great standard of living? £60,000, £100,000 per year? £200,000? Pick a number and tithe on that amount but imagine giving away 25% of the rest, or 50%, 90% or 100% above your pre-determined amount to live on. This 'heavy thought' takes some prayer, pondering and consideration. Be directed by the Holy Spirit, and you may find some explosive ideas coming to you to get you to that goal even quicker than you imagined.

It's a scary commitment, but setting your commitment level on cruise control keeps your greed level in check and your focus on becoming a kingdom person.

What would happen if each of us set a limit on the amount of money that was 'reasonable' to spend purely on us – and then gave the rest away, sowing it into kingdom purposes? Hear me out here – don't switch off just yet. Think about this: could it be that God would bless us even more abundantly if we 'pre-set' our level of contentment and didn't strive beyond it?

I know two wealthy individuals who both love God and tithe, both making millions of pounds in their respective businesses. Each is a business owner and has staff managing their operations. But there is a distinct difference between the ways they run their personal lives. I draw the following contrast not to praise or criticise either one, but to provoke your thinking.

The first person lives on just 10% of all they make and sows the remaining 90% into various kingdom endeavours. While enjoying a good lifestyle – not living like a monk – this person is very frugal about personal spending. They take the issue of stewardship very seriously and handle their resources carefully as part of their duty in serving God.

Their lifestyle is purposely simple; it is uncomplicated. Yes, they have invested in a beautiful home to live in, rental properties, investments; they have nice cars; they also go on nice holidays. Anyone viewing from the outside would love to have what they have. But, in fact they have chosen to limit their expenditure and purposefully direct their resources.

One day their son needed some new trainers. They refused to shell out £200 for a top-end pair of Michael Jordan-branded Nikes. Instead the son received a pair of perfectly good non-branded ones. They avoid needless spending and take the stewardship of money very seriously.

Several years ago, when they were not earning such a large income, they made this kind of lifestyle a goal and entered into a covenant with God regarding their finances. In the 'day of small beginnings' they embarked on the journey of living on less and giving more – frugal living, extravagant giving.

Their goal was to work towards living on 10% of their income, so each year as their income increased they increased their percentage of giving. Their desire was to be an effective conduit that money could flow through into the kingdom. The Inland Revenue has audited them several times because the government cannot believe that anyone could be so generous.

The second person also earns millions. Their lifestyle, however, is quite complicated. They own four homes on four different continents. They have a staff of thirty-seven people, including a helicopter and airline pilot on call. To meet all their personal living expenses takes around £400,000 per month.

The proposal was put to them: Would they consider capping their income and giving the rest to God? They could keep their current lifestyle but decide not to go beyond where they are now. In other words, could they set a limit on personal spending and give the rest away? The answer was no. I am not sure whether this response came out of greed or just fear of such a radical change of thinking, but the answer was still no.

It's tempting to read this and say, 'If I earned all those millions, of course I would be prepared to live on the 10%.' But would you, really? Can God trust you to be faithful with the little you have now, in order to prepare your heart to manage greater wealth in the future? If you are not doing it now, would you do it then? I'm asking you to look at this as a personal challenge and seriously consider the implications.

Self-imposed limitations, whether they are on food, sex, money or even holding your tongue, require self-discipline. Otherwise it is all too easy to fall into a self-focused 'eat, drink and be merry' way of life. In Chapter 3 we looked at the story of the rich young ruler who encountered Jesus. He left that encounter sorrowful because 'he had great riches'. I think, in reality, the great riches had him.

Making the choice to be a kingdom person with regard to our financial management is no easy choice – yet God wants to give us an abundance of wealth. He can easily get wealth *to* us, the question is: can he get it *through* us?

Jesus addressed the issue of never having enough and living a life of total self-indulgence:

> *Then he said to them, 'Watch out! Be on your guard against all kinds of greed; life does not consist in an abundance of possessions.'*
> (Luke 12:15 NIV)

Take heed and beware of covetousness (desiring something that belongs to someone else), because your life is not about how much you own. Guard against allowing your self-worth to be totally tied to your net worth. He is not saying that you cannot own possessions, just warning you not to allow the possessions to own you!

> *And he told them this parable: 'The ground of a certain rich man yielded an abundant harvest. **He** thought to **himself**, "What shall **I** do? **I** have no place to store **my** crops."*
>
> *'Then **he** said, "This is what **I'll** do. I will tear down **my** barns and build bigger ones, and there **I** will store **my** surplus grain. And **I'll** say to **myself**, '**You** have plenty of grain laid up for many years. Take life easy; eat, drink and be merry.'"*
>
> *'But God said to **him**, "**You** fool! This very night **your** life will be demanded from **you**. Then who will get what **you** have prepared for **yourself**?"*
>
> *'This is how it will be with whoever stores up things for **themselves** but is not rich toward God.'*
> (Luke 12:16–21 NIV, emphasis added)

Notice that the man 'thought to himself' without consulting God or his Word. He continues in a self-centred, egotistical vein, without considering others or having an attitude of gratitude. This is what happens when someone fails to make God the centre of their life.

God calls this man a fool. Now if you tithe and are a giver, the world will call you a fool because they don't understand biblical economics. But if you keep it and hoard it all for yourself, God calls you a fool. So, the choice is try it God's way or your own way. I would rather the world call me a fool and have God's favour.

Just before this passage, Jesus is speaking of covetousness. This rich man could not get through his head the fact that he was a 'steward' and not the actual 'owner'. He could have had so much more by letting God into the equation.

Small thinking

The unlimited wealth and vast resources at God's disposal dwarf the assets of even the wealthiest people on the planet. Bill Gates' or Warren Buffet's money is small change compared to God's fortune. We think too small; we think small is big. To a child, £20 is a lot of money, but it wouldn't make a dent in the average person's monthly budget.

We need to rise above small thinking about money and begin to tap into the heart and mind of God – the ultimate big thinker. Could the enemy have clouded our minds in order to keep us in the box of small-time thinking – lest we realise that, actually, we could fund so many more kingdom ventures than we do?

Recently, I heard a church leader say, 'I wish the church could become poor.' On the surface, this sounds like a very spiritual thing to say, but I find no scriptural basis for it. If the church was poor, how could we begin to help others who are trapped in poverty? What we need is more money accompanied by a different mind-set, a kingdom mind-set.

I wish the Church were full of debt-free, financially stable, kingdom-minded people, so that we could give from a place of abundance, not lack. If we had the members of the body of Christ living off the top of the barrel, instead of continually scraping the bottom of it, we would be living in the 'overflow' situation that God so wants for us.

Jesus said that he came to comfort the afflicted, but whenever I start speaking about money this way, people look at me as if to say, *'You've come to afflict the comfortable!'* But the heart of the issue is understanding abundance versus lack. If we truly recognised the unlimited potential of God's blessing, we wouldn't be afraid of living generous lives that are larger than ourselves.

Generosity has to be taught or preferably 'caught' from someone who is already living in the overflow. Learning how to become generous is an on-going lesson for us all, a journey on which God helps us to move forward bit by bit in trusting him implicitly. Whether we like it or not, we all tend towards selfishness.

We are capable of great, noble acts, while at the same time being capable of just the opposite. Put a person in the gutter, make them homeless and take their money away and their animal instincts come to the fore. Teach people how to become self-sufficient in their finances and to remember generosity and you have a society full of helping hands instead of closed fists.

> *The world of the generous gets larger and larger;*
> *the world of the stingy gets smaller and smaller.*
> (Proverbs 11:24, *The Message*)

As I travelled the road from poverty to having a degree of wealth, I occasionally found myself in fear of becoming homeless, penniless or both. At times desperation set in and

I had to remind myself that I serve a mighty God with unlimited resources. I had to remember that I have a Father who is committed to providing for me – who, in fact, is far more committed to me than I am to him. I had to choose to live in faith, not fear.

How much is enough?

Let's get practical. Consider your current financial position.

What would it take for you to double your current income? What cap would you need to impose on your personal spending in order to free up resources to sow into kingdom projects? Could you become a better steward of your existing resources and allow God to have his way with your finances? Get the wrecking ball out and destroy the sign over your finances saying to God: 'No entry'!

Positioning yourself as a conduit of God's blessing is not such a difficult lesson to learn if your heart is open to God's kingdom economics. Remember that Jesus said,

Give, and it will be given to you: good measure, pressed down, shaken together, and running over will be put into your bosom. For with the same measure that you use, it will be measured back to you.
(Luke 6:38)

In order to see the end result of this equation we must first take a step of faith and put something in. You must first sow a seed if you are going to reap a harvest. The way crops are produced in the natural is God's lesson to us about how life works. Sow first, reap second; keep sowing, keep reaping.

If we stop sowing, hoard what we have and don't plant, guess what happens? The harvest dries up. Do not be like the man who stood in front of his cold fireplace and said, 'As soon as I get some heat, I will put some wood on.' You have to make the first move. You need to take the first step in acknowledging God as, not just your spiritual source, but the true source of your finances. By coming into covenant with God you acknowledge him as your partner in every area of life.

When you tithe and come into covenant with God you are now in a 'joint venture' with God. He is your financial partner and you have proven it by putting him first. Included in this book is a budget for you to work through. When you realise that you and God are in partnership and you are a steward, your budget takes on a new meaning.

Why be so motivated to become a good steward over your money?

Throughout this book I have tried to encourage you to see the bigger picture when it comes to the issue of prosperity and the financial resources that God has entrusted to you. I have endeavoured to instil the truth that you possess *true riches* when you understand that:

- All you have belongs to God.
- You are God's appointed steward of your resources, but he is the owner.
- Prosperity is given by God that his people may live in the 'overflow' of his blessing and share it with others.
- Part of coming to maturity in Christ is seeing beyond ourselves: looking past our personal needs to the needs of others.

I want to challenge you to look further than your own financial concerns to see the 'resource gaps' that need filling in God's kingdom. The greatest challenge regarding money is to change your mind-set to become a generous giver, a giver not a getter, someone who is able to sow seed and expect a harvest.

I would like to share a personal testimony to remaining sensitive to God's inner direction. It is something we have to constantly keep afresh and stay tuned into. I share it with you to inspire you to be led of the Lord in your finances and especially in the area of giving.

Recently I had been looking for a nice, gently-used Mercedes to purchase, and after some research I knew that it would cost approximately £10,000. I have another vehicle but really wanted something more luxurious for travelling around the UK when on speaking engagements. I asked a friend of mine who owns a car dealership to keep an eye out for a nice used Mercedes with low mileage.

My local church has an annual offering called 'Heart for the House' – an offering that is above and beyond our tithes. I went to church knowing the offering was being received that day, and had predetermined an amount to give. When the offering was received I put in the amount I had set aside. As I put the money in the bucket I felt the Holy Spirit ask me, 'Do you really need that car? Why not put that amount in for this offering?'

Now, I remember the first time I felt this leading of God to give a large amount of money, I said, 'I rebuke you, devil! Get away from me!' Then I began to realise that small inner voice that leads us in the spirit was simply testing my willingness and sensitivity to God's leading.

So, back to the story. I said, 'Lord, I really do not need the Mercedes and think this amount for the Heart for the House offering will go to do some greater things than me driving a Mercedes. No problem!'

I gave the £10,000 that day and was totally happy to wait

for the car. I did not give to get, I gave because I believed in the cause the money was going to.

Now, I still had money to go and buy another car, but I am very disciplined when it comes to setting money aside for a trip or any item. (It is part of the fun of setting goals and reaching them.)

I went home and totally forgot about the situation, resolved to wait and get the car at some other time.

On Tuesday I received a call from a friend of mine. He told me he had heard I was looking for a nice used Mercedes and inquired whether I had purchased one yet.

'No, I've not bought one yet,' I responded.

'Great! I have a Mercedes someone just gave me and I want to bless you with it!'

I have been a tither for years and have given away cars but never received one, and I am not saying that if you give you will get a Mercedes. That is not my point.

I do not understand how sowing and reaping works! All I can attest to is it does work. If you sow a seed, eventually you will reap. Maybe not three days after you give as in this story, but I do know God's principles in the natural and spiritual on sowing and reaping work!

Once you have set in place the foundation of tithing, consider giving to some causes that you believe in. Look at the causes your local church support and consider giving to one of them.

In the UK there are over 150,000 charities. There are so many good causes and so many needs to be met. This should motivate us to make a difference in the world by contributing to causes we believe in.

Below is a list of some of the charities I support. I love charities that help people to turn their lives around and raise them out of poverty, which promote independence and increase people's self-worth and self-respect. I also favour charities that help families and children.

Determine to become someone who does more than just make money. Life is bigger than that. Become someone who is financially independent and able to sow into the lives of others.

- **Habitat for Humanity** (building homes for under-privileged families) – www.habitatforhumanity.org.uk
- **Compassion** (changing a child's life; it will enrich you and the child) – www.compassionuk.org
- **World Vision** (child sponsorship and more) – www.worldvision.org.uk
- **Kiva** (microfinance for entrepreneurs around the world) – www.kiva.org
- **Heifer Project** (supplying farm animals to poor families) – www.heifer.org
- **A21 Campaign** (setting people free from the slave trade) – www.thea21campaign.org
- **I Care Revolution** (challenging injustice) – www.icarerevolution.com

Trimming the fat

So why am I so obsessed or focused on living below my means and saving money? I call it 'trimming the fat' or excess out of my budget. It could be saving money on my utilities or on my home insurance that helps trim the fat and save money.

£25 per month savings on your budget may not seem like a great deal, but this could sponsor a child with Compassion to send them to school, feed and clothe them. £25 per month in an investment over 25 years is only £7,500 saved but in a good fund at 6% return it will turn into £18,000. This money could be put to better use in either your pocket or in one of your favourite causes.

Every time I do a financial transaction, I ask myself how I can be a good steward of that money. I love seeing lives changed and it takes money to do that.

£25 a month helps get a young woman out of sex slavery.

£25 a month buys a heifer and chickens and sets up a small farmer in a third-world country to become self-sufficient.

£25 a month helps a family to build their own house.

£25 a month can change lives. I can't fund all the charities, but I can do something.

Together if we each do our part we can make the world a better place.

Look at how to 'trim the fat' and eliminate unnecessary expenses. Ask yourself in each category, 'Is this really a necessity?'

For example, gym membership costs on average £35 per month. If you owe money on a credit card, cancel the gym and use the £35 to start paying off your credit card debt. Put on a pair of trainers and run outside – it is free!

Look at the Budget – Fat Finder chart on pages 125–126. Get focused on learning how to implement frugal living, extravagant giving and help change the world. This is prosperity with purpose.

BUDGET – FAT FINDER

INCOME	Weekly	Monthly		
Combined Total Income (inc. Benefits)				
COMBINED TOTAL INCOME		£		

HOUSEHOLD			Can Reduce to	Total Savings
Mortgage/Rent				
Council Tax/Service Charge				
Electricity				
Gas				
Water Rates				
Home Phone and Internet				
Household/Garden Maintenance				
Mobile Phone(s)				
Shopping – Bulk (Food, Toiletries, etc.)				
Shopping – Extras weekly (Bread, Milk, etc.)				
Other (Insert Name)				
HOUSEHOLD TOTAL		£		
HOUSEHOLD TOTAL SAVINGS				£

INSURANCE				
Building and Contents				
Car Insurance(s)				
Life Insurance(s)				
Private Health Care/Health Insurance				
Pet Insurance				
Travel Insurance				
Credit Card Payment Protection				
Mortgage Protection				
Other Insurance (Insert Name)				
INSURANCE CURRENT TOTAL		£		
INSURANCE TOTAL SAVINGS				£

CARD & LOAN REPAYMENTS				
Debt(s) Combined				
DEBT TOTAL		£		

SAVINGS				
Savings (inc. Pension, ISAs, Trust, Stocks, etc.)				
SAVINGS CURRENT TOTAL		£		

TRAVEL				
Petrol/Diesel				
Road Tax				
Parking				
Breakdown Cover				
Oyster Card/Travel Card				
Other (Insert Name)				
TRAVEL CURRENT TOTAL		£		
TRAVEL TOTAL SAVINGS				£

BUDGET – FAT FINDER

FOOD & DRINK	Weekly	Monthly	Can Reduce to	Total Savings
Meals/Snacks/Beverages Partner 1				
Meals/Snacks/Beverages Partner 2				
FOOD & DRINK CURRENT TOTAL		£		
FOOD & DRINK TOTAL SAVINGS				£
LEISURE				
Socialising/Nights Out				
Alcohol				
Smoking				
TV Licence				
Satellite/Cable, etc.				
Other (Insert Name)				
LEISURE CURRENT TOTAL		£		
LEISURE TOTAL SAVINGS				£
CHILDCARE				
Child Maintenance				
Childcare/Babysitting/Nursery				
School Meals				
Children's Activities/Hobbies				
Pocket Money				
Other (Insert Name)				
CHILDCARE CURRENT TOTAL		£		
CHILDCARE TOTAL SAVINGS				£
HEALTH & BEAUTY				
Gym Membership/Other Recreation				
Haircut – His				
Hairdressing – Hers				
Beauty Treatment (inc. Nails, Facials, etc.)				
Beauty Products				
Other (Insert Name)				
HEALTH & BEAUTY CURRENT TOTAL		£		
HEALTH & BEAUTY TOTAL SAVINGS				£
MISCELLANEOUS				
New Clothes				
Newspaper/Magazine				
Tithing/Charity				
Other (Insert Name)				
MISCELLANEOUS CURRENT TOTAL		£		
MISCELLANEOUS TOTAL SAVINGS				£
SUMMARY				
TOTAL MONTHLY INCOME	£			
TOTAL MONTHLY EXPENDITURE		£		
TOTAL MONTHLY SAVINGS (FAT FOUND)				£

CHAPTER 9

Developing a Practical Financial Plan

Over the years I have found that many people have faith but lack facts about how to implement their vision for the future. I hope that this book has enlightened you and challenged you to see things from a different perspective. Learning these things biblically and practically is a journey for everyone.

Now, let us jump in and learn how to do some practical things. Many of the things I will cover in the practical aspects are common sense, but you will see that they are not common knowledge and certainly not common practice.

'My people are destroyed for lack of knowledge.'
(Hosea 4:6)

The converse of this is that God's people prosper with an abundance of knowledge.

I began in business at the age of nineteen. I struggled along in sales for the next few years until, aged twenty-four, I went to a financial seminar that radically changed my thinking. What I learnt blew my mind. The speaker gave us sound wealth-generation principles and offered to create a financial game plan for anyone who wanted one. I signed up immediately and my game plan, based on the five principles we will look at below, became like a navigation system to me.

When my first assessment was done, I was quite encouraged. The plan had totalled up all my assets and deducted my liabilities and the result was $10,000 net worth. I thought this was pretty good until my wife, Margo, dug me in the ribs and pointed out that there was actually a minus sign in front of that figure.

We were, in fact, worth –$10,000. With a practical plan to move things forward, combined with an increasing understanding of the biblical principles of prosperity, things began to change for the better.

Getting educated about money

It never ceases to amaze me that schools do not teach young kids anything about financial management. Maths did not make any sense to me at school and unfortunately my fourth grade teacher one day asked me, 'Are you stupid or something?' Later, however, under the tutelage of a great mentor, finance began to make perfect sense to me and when a dollar or pound sign went in front of a number it took over a new and practical meaning.

Most young people leave the education system with little financial training and enter the big world of work with a certain amount of naivety. They get a job and, seized by the novelty of suddenly having some money, they begin to spend. It seems we need no education on spending money! From there it is easy to get onto the *work–earn–spend* treadmill, keep your head down and never look up.

Like many people of that age, at twenty-four I had no clue where I was heading. Sure, I was working hard, but I had no real plan. I was working in finance and Margo was teaching in school, but though we were both earning, our outgoings exceeded our income. We were slowly going broke for lack of a plan. We were perishing for lack of knowledge.

Developing a financial game plan was a wake-up call for me – mostly from a spiritual standpoint. Among other things, I realised that I was not being a good steward over my money, so I studied more about what the Bible had to say and sought to gain a financial education.

Previously I have mentioned that I found a great mentor to help me. I realise that not everyone will be fortunate enough to have that, but in this chapter I want to share a number of the important principles I learned to guide you onto the right track. I would also like to encourage you to attend financial seminars and become better informed. At the end of the book I will give ideas about getting this practical education.

After creating a personal game plan and setting certain goals, I focused on putting the plan into action. I started working part-time in a financial education business and in the first year I made around $28,000 working 10–15 hours per week. My first priority was to pay my tithe; my second was to pay off my high-interest credit card debt. By the end of that first year, aged twenty-five, I was debt-free, apart from my property mortgage.

My second year in business I left my job and went full time into the business I had been doing part-time. That second year I doubled my income but we maintained the same lifestyle and saved $20,000. I realised I had to build my own financial house first with a sturdy foundation before

I could really have 'overflow' to give. Going into my third year we were making a great income, with no personal debt, low expenses and money in the savings account. Life was good.

Margo and I discussed 'stepping out in faith' now that we had a solid foundation of finances. We were already tithing but we felt a nudge from the Lord to do more.

Our local church had remodelled the year before and had a $50,000 mortgage which they were repaying at $1,000 per month. We approached the pastor and volunteered to take over the payment. I think it was the only time in my twelve years at the church that he did not need to pray about something!

In nine months we had the entire debt paid off and my income doubled again that year and doubled again the following year! Coincidence? I think not.

This action and step of faith was an outward sign that God could trust me to let money flow through me. A few years after this incident, I had become a millionaire. How? hard work, right opportunities and the blessing of God. Through the years I learned that generosity makes you wealthy on the inside and giving helps you to prosper in every area of your life!

I believe that this act of acknowledging God in my finances and living out Matthew 6:33 (NIV):

Seek first his kingdom and his righteousness, and all these things will be given to you as well.

Thirty years on, I have never been in debt since, except for a mortgage on a property or an investment property. When you tithe consistently and handle your finances wisely, you cannot help but be blessed.

One of the saddest scriptures in the Bible is Luke 16:8: '. . . *the children of this world . . . are wiser than the children of the light.*'

It is high time that the children of light wised up for the kingdom. Be wise, learn how to maximise your resources, and allow God's Word to teach you how to be a generous giver.

You need to build a financial plan and, in so doing, I believe God will bless your efforts. Here I want to share with you five practical principles you can use to build a solid financial game plan for your future.

Building Your Financial House

Like any proper structure, the building must have a good foundation. When building your Financial House you must begin from the ground up.

Top Floor: Income Management

Third Floor: Asset Management

Second Floor: Expense Management

First Floor: Debt Management

The Foundation: Risk Management

Get a plan and write it down

In Matthew 7:24–27, Jesus told a parable about two men who both built houses. One built his house on shifting sand, while the other laid a firm foundation on solid rock. You'll recall, when the storms came, which house remained standing.

Developing a solid financial game plan is much like building a house and you can think of the following five principles in this way: first you lay a foundation, then you build successive floors, and finally you cover it over with a watertight roof.

What do you need before you build a house? A plan. Unless an architect draws up some plans, you could just go out and start digging a trench for the foundation and end up with a mess. It is amazing that most people spend more time planning a holiday with the family than they do their financial house.

So, the first step is to sit down and write down some goals for your life. Where do you want your life to be in one year, five years, ten years, or twenty years?

Write the vision
And make it plain on tablets . . .
(Habakkuk 2:2)

And

Take delight in the LORD,
  and he will give you the desires of your heart.
(Psalm 37:4 NIV)

I hear people say 'I only want what God wants for me.' Now, that sounds really spiritual but it's not biblical if you're too passive about it. What do you want for your future? Have you written it down and made it plain? If you do not know what you want and have no concrete goals you will, by default, never achieve them.

How close are you to achieving your life goals and dreams? I'm a big believer in having what I call a CCMP – a Clear Concise Mental Picture. You can set goals for every area of your life – spiritual goals, health goals, relationship goals and financial goals – then work towards achieving them.

Write your goals down, otherwise they can be nebulous and you can easily lose track of your progress. The first step is to get a plan in writing.

It's interesting that only 5% of people have their goals for the future written down and read them regularly. It's also interesting that only 5% of people at age 65 are financially independent and 95% are broke or still working – and not by choice! I doubt that I will ever retire (Why should I? I love what I do!) but it sure is nice to have a choice and not be forced to continue to work because of an inadequate income. Could there be a link here of people not having their goals clearly defined and people not being financially secure?

Five key principles of a financial game plan for your future

1. *Protection*
The foundation of your financial game plan is to ensure that you have adequate insurance cover in place to safeguard against the unknowns of life. There are certain things that, legally, we are obliged to have insurance for: our car and our property if it is mortgaged. But although we are not bound by law to have life insurance and business insurance, we have to consider whether we need them.

If you are young and single, then life insurance is probably not a necessity and that money would be better going into savings or investments. If you are married and have a family, however, then life cover is essential in order to provide for your family, should anything happen to you. It's like renting wealth until you can actually have the real money in savings.

If you own a business I would suggest that you get proper business protection too. Because I run a business we have proper protection in place to cover any potential problems. I hope we never have to use it, but that is what insurance is for.

> *The prudent see danger and take refuge,*
> *but the simple keep going and pay the penalty.*
> (Proverbs 22:3 NIV)

Be prudent, be smart and plan for the future. As I mentioned, if you are married, have children, and have certain fixed expenses then it is wise to have a back-up plan in place should anything happen to you. No one, least of all Christians, likes to think that anything bad will happen. But that's not how life works.

I have seen too many unexpected tragedies not to pass on this guidance. My own father committed suicide and left our family penniless, so I have seen the results first hand. Let me be clear, having such protection is not a denial of faith – it is being responsible. It is being a good steward of those you love that God has placed under your care.

The Apostle Paul endorsed this principle when he gave his son in the faith, Timothy, the following sound advice:

> *If anyone does not provide for his own, and especially for those*
> *of his household, he has denied the faith and is worse than an*
> *unbeliever.*
> (1 Timothy 5:8)

And Solomon wrote that,

> *Sensible people will see trouble coming and avoid it, but an*
> *unthinking person will walk right into it and regret it later.*
> (Proverbs 22:3 GNT)

Most people don't have the cash reserves necessary to provide for their family if they are no longer around, so insurance cover is a good way of providing an 'instant estate' that will take care of them in the future. This could be in the form of life cover, critical illness cover or any policy that produces a lump sum in the event of premature death or long-term sickness.

People often ask me, 'When is the best time to buy life cover?' If I knew the future then I would say, 'The day before you die.' But since none of us know when that will be, the answer must be *now*.

Here are some startling statistics for you:

- 1 in 4 men currently aged twenty-five will not live to the age of sixty-five.
- 1 in 5 adults have a mortgage with no associated life cover.
- Over 55% of all critical illness claims are for cancer and 1 in 3 people in the UK will develop some form of cancer in their lives.

I don't want to scare you into action with statistics, because I do not want anyone to walk in fear. But I do want to encourage you to be prepared and make adequate provision for the future, whatever it may hold.

The foundation of any financial game plan, then, is to prepare for the unforeseen future. For a very modest amount of money it is amazing how much cover you can have, and that will give you incredible peace of mind.

2. Debt management
A good financial game plan will work towards a position of debt freedom. We have already discussed how no verses in the Bible suggest debt is a good thing.

Paul said,

Owe no one anything . . .
(Romans 13:8)

And Solomon declared,

The borrower is servant to the lender.
(Proverbs 22:7)

Debt is like a noose around your neck and it creates nothing but pressure and stress – especially when it comes to high-interest credit card debt. When I was twenty-four I had $10,000 of credit card and car loan debt and I got sucked into the 'easy monthly payments' trap, paying extortionate amounts of interest. If you have credit card debt, it should be your number one priority to get rid of it as quickly as possible.

Whatever it is that you think you must have now, stop and re-evaluate it. Whether it's that new pair of shoes, a suit or dress, that holiday, or whatever, do not rush ahead and buy it on credit. You will end up paying much more for it than you wanted to.

In order to speed up the process of becoming debt-free, you can take action to sell the things you don't actually need. Most people have a loft or a garage full of stuff they hardly ever touch. Why not sell it on eBay?

Do you have lots of books? You can sell them on Amazon. I have sat with families who had thousands of pounds of credit card debt and suggested they go through their book collection and dispose of anything non-essential. I have seen people wipe out their credit cards by selling a bunch of books they were unlikely to read ever again.

I also know of some families whose young children are making extra money buying and selling used books! Consider getting a part-time job or business to make an extra income to get out of debt quicker.

Ten years ago Margo and I ventured into the loft of our house and found box after box of 'stuff'. We sorted through them all, looking at each other and asking, 'Why on *earth did we buy this?*'

We had a major clear out and either sold, gave away or threw away every bit of excess.

There is so much freedom in living a simple life. Often we buy things because they are the equivalent of comfort food. It's called retail therapy. Rarely do you really need to spend that money and you certainly should not go into debt to do it. Instead, focus on working your way out of debt and into financial freedom.

I do not believe anyone can enjoy total financial freedom unless they are free from debt. Scarcely a day goes by when the news does not feature another aspect of the global economic crisis and very few people remain untouched by it.

Just five years ago people thought they were invincible: they went crazy buying investment properties without really knowing what they were doing. Now redundancy rates are up, VAT is up, university fees have trebled, gas and electricity prices are going up, the threshold for 40% income tax has been lowered and benefits are down. The people who are hurting the most are those who are trying to juggle high-interest debt on credit cards or one of the many 'payday loan' companies that have astronomical interest rates.

Nobody plans to fail financially, but they fail to plan. So the first step towards financial freedom is to eradicate your debt and begin to accumulate some savings. This way, when the unexpected happens, you will be prepared.

3. Expense management

A great goal to set before addressing other issues is to accumulate at least £1,000 in savings. Although it may not sound like much, it will actually give you incredible peace of mind. Then, if any emergency occurs, you know you have a contingency plan.

After that, turn your attention to how you will manage your expenses. By this I mean planning and executing a budget based on your income that includes a 10% tithe as a priority. I have already stressed my belief in the principle of tithing.

I have a simple method that I have used for years that determines how much goes where. It is called the 10-10-10-70 principle. It determines what percentage of your income goes into short or long-term savings and how much you live off. When you look at this method, you may be tempted to think, 'I can't do that.' But I firmly believe it is achievable for everyone, regardless of your level of income, and will produce positive, tangible results.

There is a simple budgeting method you can use to govern how much goes into these three areas. The first 10% of your income is your tithe. The next 10% goes into your emergency fund and short-term savings. 10% goes into a long-term investment plan and then you live (and give) off of the remaining 70%.

I admit that it is difficult to do this if you are working towards financial freedom from a position of debt. So you must start where you are and progress with this goal in mind. When I began, I paid my 10% tithe but saved only £25 per month, because I was using the balance to pay off my debt that was at 18–24% interest. The longer I worked at it, though, the more my financial position improved by applying this simple principle.

Your goal for your emergency fund should be to build up

the equivalent of three to six months' living expenses. It will give you the peace of mind that, should something unexpected happen, such as losing your job, you will not be plunged into an immediate crisis. So many people allow no margin for the unexpected. This is not good stewardship.

4. Asset management

In plain terms, asset management is putting a proportion of your income to work in short and long-term investment portfolios. The first suggestion I want to give you here is: do not be tempted to jump into this unless you have completed the previous three steps. You cannot move to XYZ unless you have gone past ABC!

Here the biblical principle applies of being faithful with a little before moving on to handling larger amounts of money. If you are a good steward of your resources, having responsibly taken any necessary protective measures, worked to get out of debt, and sought to control your spending, then I believe God will bless you as you seek to create some long term investments.

Many experts agree that you should put a percentage of your net income into savings – usually around 10%. But if you want to have a complete savings programme, then I believe you need to have three accounts:

- An emergency account.
- A short-term savings account.
- A long-term investment account.

The 10-10-10-70 plan

Using a bank account as part of a long-term savings strategy, as many people do, is a guaranteed loss-making exercise. Look at the following example:

Say you invest £10,000 in a savings account that returns 4% interest. At the end of one year you will pay £80 in tax on your interest and, if you are in a 20% income tax bracket, you will now have £10,320. But, due to inflation of 3.5% (£361 on a sum of £10,320), your net purchasing power is just £9,958.80, so in real terms you are making a loss of £41.20. I call that going broke safely.

A bank is fine for short-term savings, due to its easy accessibility, but is not the right vehicle for a long-term investment plan. We need to look at alternatives.

5. Income Management

If the previous steps were the foundation and various floors of the house, income management is the roof. If your boss were to call you into his office tomorrow and say, 'It's bad news; I'm sorry but I have to make you redundant,' would that spell financial disaster for you or would you be well covered? Most people are only one or two pay-cheques away from disaster, firstly because they live beyond their means, and secondly because they have not thought to plan for such an eventuality.

You wouldn't want to drive around in a car that had no spare tyre, or a flat spare tyre, would you? So why have no contingency plan when it comes to your work? My suggestion is to look for ways to develop other income streams, so that you are not simply at the mercy of your job.

There are numbers of options available for creating a second income, without working yourself into the ground. I love the teaching of my friend, Rabbi Daniel Lapin, on this topic. In his simple, but profound, way he says that all you need to do to start your own business is to find a need that people want met and work out a creative way of serving them to fulfil it. I highly recommend his book *Thou Shall Prosper*.

This is a wonderfully biblical approach. Look at the example of the apostles. Although they were in full-time ministry, they generated their own support from alternative income streams. Paul ran a tent-making business.

Peter had built up a fishing business. As I already said, I do not believe that when he followed Jesus he simply abandoned his business and left his boats and nets to rot on the beach. It is much more likely that he put someone else in charge of running the business or rented out his boats and nets to other fisherman, so that he could continue to draw an income to take care of his living expenses.

We can be creative about how we generate extra income for ourselves and God will bless that as we continue to maintain a generous, giving heart. Have you ever considered doing something in your spare time to generate a second income stream? Robert Kiyosaki, in his book *Rich Dad, Poor Dad*, talks about the benefits of becoming a business owner.

Typically, when you work for someone else they pay you just enough so that you do not quit your job and go somewhere else. I am not suggesting that you resign tomorrow and launch a business, but the fact is, everyone has God-given skills and talents that could be put to use in a business enterprise.

It could be carpentry, sewing, counselling or coaching; everyone has 'seed' they can sow. Everyone has a gift related to their passion that could, if applied, be turned into pounds to generate a new income stream alongside their existing job. Many people hate their day jobs, so why not do something you love that people need and create a business out of it?

In my own financial services company, Genistar, we have many people who work part time and have built up a residual or 'passive' income of around £1,000 per month. In other words they have already put in the hard work and now it is generating an on-going income. We have several people who have even found their new-found business venture at Genistar to be a whole new career and have made the transition from their old job to a new and exciting career helping coach people on their finances. My point is, whatever you can do, consider generating a new income stream in this way. Think outside the box. Times have changed and so must you.

To sum up
I hope you have been challenged to look at things from a different perspective and to get into the Scriptures and search deeper into what God's Word says about money. There are thousands of scriptures that speak about money. This book is in no way a fully comprehensive study on biblical economics. There is so much more to learn.

Acts 17:11 (NIV) says,

> *[the Berean Jews] received the message with great eagerness and examined the Scriptures every day to see if what Paul said was true.*

I challenge you to stay sensitive to the Holy Spirit, to keep an open heart and mind, and search the Scriptures. I hope you have been challenged to look at things from a different perspective.

The thoughts, ideas and concepts in this book I have shared with you have been what I have personally learned over thirty-five years in finance and studying biblical economics.

Hopefully the title *True Riches* now makes sense to you in your own journey to having God's total shalom and peace in all four areas of your life. It is a juggling act to get these four areas all 'in sync' but it is possible. Finances affect every other area of our lives and once you get this area settled all the other pieces of the puzzle seem to fall in place.

I pray that you develop to your full potential, live life to the fullest and stretch yourself to the outer limits of success. God has a plan for your life, and it is an awesome plan!

Jeffrey Lestz

Afterword

The best time to plan for your financial future was twenty years ago; the second best time is now!

How may we be of service to you?

If you have a further interest in getting more information on biblical economics or on one of our financial courses please email us at jefflestz.pa@genistar.org.

Visit me at www.jefflestz.co.uk

 **@jeffreylestz**

www.facebook.com/jefflestz